DOUG STANTON

GOOD DAD BAD DAD

2024 by Douglas J Stanton

ISBN: 9798334584624 (paperback)

All Scripture quotations, unless otherwise indicated, are from the Holy Bible, New. International Version®, NIV®. Copyright ©1973, 1978, 1984, 2011 by Biblical, Inc.TM
Used by permission of Zondervan. All rights reserved worldwide. www.-zondervan.com. The "NIV" and "New International Version" are trademarks registered in the United States Patent and Trademark Office by Biblical, Inc.TM
Scripture quotations marked NASB1995 are from the (NASB®) New American Standard Bible®, Copyright © 1960, 1971, 1977, 1995 by The Lockman Foundation.
Used by permission. All rights reserved. www.lockman.org.
News Publishers. Used by permission. All rights reserved.
Scripture quotations marked NLT are from the Holy Bible, New Living Translation, copyright ©1996, 2004, 2015 by Tyndale House Foundation. Used by permission of Tyndale House Publishers, a Division of Tyndale House Ministries, Carol Stream, Illinois 60188. All rights reserved.
Scripture quotations marked MSG are from THE MESSAGE, copyright © 1993, 2002,
2018 by Eugene H. Peterson. Used by permission of NavPress. All rights reserved. Represented by Tyndale House Publishers, a Division of Tyndale House Ministries.
Scripture quotations marked NKJV are from the New King James Version®.
Copyright © 1982 by Thomas Nelson. Used by permission. All rights reserved.
Scripture quotations marked KJV are from the King James Version of the Bible. Public
domain.
Scripture quotations marked AMP are from the Amplified® Bible (AMP), copyright ©
2015 by The Lockman Foundation. Used by permission. www.lockman.org.
All emphasis in Scripture is the author's. Scripture quotations marked ESV are from the ESV® Bible (The Holy Bible, English
Standard Version®), copyright © 2001 by Crossway, a publishing ministry of Good

CONTENTS

Endorsements
Introduction

1. The Role Of A Father.   13
2. Dads In The Bible   25
3. God's Balanced Home   43
4. Meaningful Communication   55
5. Media And Children   63
6. A Fatherless Generation   73
7. A Father To The Fatherless   79
8. Father Figure For The Fatherless   87
9. Male Role Models   97
10. Story Of A Bad Dad   107
11. Childhood Trauma   115
12. Nothing Impossible For My Dad   127
13. Love Voids   135
14.The Message Of The Cross   141
15.Power Of Forgiveness   151
16.Empty Nesters   163
17.EPILOGUE   169
18. INFORMATION   173

ENDORSEMENTS

Deep within the follower of Christ is a God-given desire for more. The problem is that this desire is so often quickly suppressed because "life happens." Daily distractions seem to capture our thoughts, and instead of focusing on heaven, we find our minds set on "earth." What is desperately needed is a "voice" that can call out and awaken us to our current condition and release within us a hunger for God's presence once again. We need a voice that will reawaken us to the longing we once had and restore us to our awareness of God's powerful love. We need a voice that will speak into the depths of our hearts and call us to the reality of "Christ in us, the hope of glory."

I thank God for using Doug Stanton as that voice in my own life. I remember the moment when I first heard the passion for revival that came from his heart and it immediately resonated with my own. Ever since that time, I personally have had a greater hunger for something that cannot be satisfied with anything other than the fullness of the Holy Spirit. I have also seen the release of a corporate,

united desire for a regional, transforming move of God's presence as more and more are renewed in seeking a revival that can only come from the
heart of the Father.

Pastor Mike Smith
Redeeming Love Church, Maplewood, MN
(Mike Smith is a City Father who has an incredible heart for the whole Twin Cities area of Minnesota, not just his church. He is chaplain to the local government, is highly respected by all, and has been a personal friend and a great support to Doug and Karen.)

Doug Stanton came for a week's ministry here in the Twin Cities in 1995, and has been here, so to speak, ever since. He has done more to foster revival in individual people's lives and churches these last twenty years than anyone else I know. He brought a fresh experience of the Holy Spirit that was marked by signs, wonders, and miracles.

But probably one of the biggest things that I noticed was that he was used to revitalize the spiritual life of so many people who testified of a renewed relationship with the Lord. I know many people who are fervently serving the Lord now and who trace their renewal of life in the Spirit to their involvement in Doug Stanton's ministry.

Doug was spontaneous in what he did. No pre-programmed

message or ministry. He just brought the Word that he sensed God was giving him at the moment and moved as the Holy Spirit led him.

He is loving, sensitive, and patient in the way he ministers to
individuals. He never seemed to be in a hurry, often ministering long into the night as people waited to receive ministry and prayer. Doug was blessed to be supported in ministry by his wife, Karen, and their children contributed to the praise and worship. It became a family affair.

Doug has overcome many times of testing and teaches from experience. Doug gave of himself physically as he ministered night after night, seven nights a week. He is very ecumenical and was able to minister alongside, encourage, and help ministers from all different backgrounds. Doug is always Christ-centered and, like Paul, it was a case of proclaiming Christ and declaring, "Christ, in you the hope of glory."

Pastor Alan Langstaff

(Alan Langstaff *is an Australian-born apostle now based in the United States. He is on the board of significant ministries around the world and is a Father in the Twin Cities of Minnesota. He has been Doug's pastor in the United States, and he and his wife, Dorothy, are close personal friends of Doug and Karen.*)

I have known Doug Stanton since I was a teenager. I consider him one of my closest mentors and friends. The wealth of wisdom that he has from all the places God has taken him all over the world is completely invaluable. It's astounding the amount of patience and compassion that this man has had over all these decades. Always consistent and always willing to change if need be. This has been a bright light in this era for me, to see the life of Christ lived out through Doug. Honestly, I see Christ, the hope of glory, in Doug. This
book offers life experiences married with Scripture to show the life that wins by following Christ. Through the ups and downs and through everyday pressure, this book offers comfort and, at the same time, some fatherly instruction on how to overcome in life.

I recommend this book to everyone. It will bring you closer to
God through a personal relationship with Jesus Christ through His Holy Spirit. You will be inspired, moved, and greatly challenged, and in the end, you will be changed.

Roy Fields
Run With Fire Ministries
(Roy Fields is the founder and president of Run With Fire Ministries. He is a spiritual son of Doug's by his choice. Doug and his family have been blessed to be Roy's friends and cherish their times with Melanie and Roy.)

7

Good Dad Bad Dad

INTRODUCTION

Understanding Fatherhood in a Fatherless Generation

A father's influence, whether good or bad, has a monumental effect on a person's ability to face life, relationships in family and marriage, and relate to God as a father.

I have helped thousands of people face and understand the damage that has created love voids in their lives. The first step in facing these soul-damaging effects in a person's life is to be aware of the loss of a father's love, protection, and nourishment in their lives. There are so many dysfunctional families that make this obvious, but the loss of a balanced father's love and involvement in an individual's life is not always apparent in a seemingly normal family.

In this book, I endeavor to speak to this issue with my years of personal experience that has helped thousands of men, women, and children overcome this massive disadvantage to have a fruitful and happy relationship with God and family.

I have chosen the name of this book, 'Good Dad Bad Dad,' to accentuate the extremes between a dad who brings forth good fruit and a dad who brings forth bad fruit. Even as you read this, you probably reflect on your dad and your relationship with him or lack thereof, depending on your circumstances. If you are a dad, you have probably already judged yourself as a good dad or a bad or average dad.

The impact of a father figure on a child's development is profound and multifaceted. The presence of a good dad can foster a nurturing environment, instilling confidence and security in children. A positive dad influence often translates into better emotional control, improved social skills, and higher academic achievement. Children with engaged fathers tend to develop healthier relationships and exhibit lower levels of behavioral problems.

In comparison, the effects of a bad dad can be equally significant but in detrimental ways. An absent or neglectful father may contribute to feelings of abandonment, low self-esteem, and difficulty forming trusting relationships later in life. Children raised in such environments may struggle with emotional issues and face challenges in their interactions.

Moreover, the absence of any father figure can create a void that affects children profoundly. While many single-parent families thrive with strong maternal (mother) support, the lack of paternal (father) guidance can lead to increased risks for behavioral issues and academic struggles. Ultimately, whether it's through positive engagement or harmful neglect, the role of dads —good or bad—shapes the trajectory of their children's lives in critical ways that deserve our attention and understanding.

The sad reality is that children have no choice about parental influence. Broken homes, accidents, and sickness that contribute to the loss of a father's influence are becoming more common in our world.

I want to explore the many ways a person can be affected by good or bad dad experiences, as well as possible solutions and ways to help restore everyday life by overcoming the past and its long-term effects.

Good Dad Bad Dad

CHAPTER ONE

The Role of a Father

The role of a father is one of the most significant and multifaceted positions in a child's life. Fathers are not just providers; they are mentors, protectors, and emotional anchors. A father's influence shapes a child's development, instilling values that last a lifetime. I assume, even by reading so far, you have considered the role your dad played in your life and the possible effects that you are coping with in day-to-day life and relationships. Remember, I am sharing these things as a mirror to help you overcome what has disadvantaged you.

I have often shared in my meetings that I had a great dad who shaped me and helped me in countless ways to face the challenges that followed my upbringing. He was and still is my hero. It wasn't until I began to support and counsel others that I truly realized how special my dad was to me. The stark contrast between my experiences and those of many people I encountered left me shocked in my early ministry.

I found many individuals carry the weight of absent or dysfunctional parental figures, which profoundly affects their confidence, decision-making, and overall outlook on life. Through these conversations over the years, it became clear that a supportive father can be a cornerstone for personal development and resilience in a child's life. My dad's unwavering guidance instilled in me values of integrity, hard work, and compassion—qualities that have not only propelled me forward but also allowed me to uplift others. Was my dad perfect? No, he was not, and my brothers may not even share the same opinion of our dad, but my experiences with my dad shaped my life and, in many ways, my personality and stature.

As I reflect on this realization, it's evident that the role of a father extends far beyond mere presence; it's about active engagement and emotional support. As a pastor, this understanding has motivated me to advocate for strong family bonds and highlight the importance of positive role models in our families. Let us cherish those who shape us positively while recognizing the profound impact we can have on those close to us by simply being present in their lives.

My dad was a very practical man who grew up on a farm with eight siblings. It seemed to me as a young boy that my dad could do anything as he applied himself to it. He had a saying, " If you have a lever long enough and a fulcrum strong enough, you could move the flaming world." I am sure his dad said that in his hearing, and my kids had heard me say that when they wondered if dad could build or fix something we faced as a family.

Research consistently shows that children with involved fathers tend to have better social skills, higher self-esteem, and improved academic performance. This is no coincidence. A father's presence provides a sense of security and stability that fosters confidence and resilience in children.

Personally, because I had a very hands-on dad, he played an instrumental role in shaping my brothers' and my futures. His active involvement in our lives went beyond being present; he engaged with us in meaningful ways that equipped us for the challenges ahead. From teaching us essential life skills to instilling values of responsibility and resilience, my father understood the importance of preparing us for the life that was ahead of us.

He spent countless hours with us, fixing things around the house, working on the farm, helping fix our bikes and eventually our cars, or simply having deep conversations about life choices. These experiences were not just bonding moments; they were lessons that laid a solid foundation for adulthood. As we reached the age to leave our parents' home, we felt ready—not because we had memorized facts from textbooks but because we had learned how to navigate the complexities of life through practical experience.

I believe this hands-on approach is invaluable and should be embraced by all parents. It fosters independence and confidence in children, ensuring they are well-equipped to face the world independently. My father's commitment to being actively present has left an indelible mark on our lives, reinforcing that actual parenting goes beyond providing; it involves engaging deeply with your children's growth and development.

Parent Replaced Lifestyles

In our modern, fast-paced world, it has become increasingly common for both parents to juggle demanding careers while relying on babysitters and childcare facilities to care for their children. This shift, driven by the rising cost of living and an insatiable desire for more—whether it's material possessions or career advancements—often comes at a significant cost to the well-being of our children.

When parents are stretched thin between work commitments and the pressures of daily life, it's the youngest members of our families who may suffer. The emotional connection that is vital during a child's formative years can be compromised when caregivers are not present. While professional childcare providers can offer safety and supervision, they cannot replace the nurturing bond that comes from parental involvement.

Moreover, many childcare facilities operate under strict schedules, prioritizing efficiency over individual attention. Children thrive in environments where they feel seen and heard; however, in busy daycare settings, this personal touch can often be lost. As parents strive to provide a better life through their hard work, we must ask ourselves: at what point does this pursuit come at the expense of our children's emotional health?

Ultimately, while both parents working is often necessary in today's economic landscape, it's crucial to evaluate how we can balance these demands with quality time spent with our children. Prioritizing family connections amidst busy schedules should not just be an afterthought; it should be central to how we define success as families in today's world. I am sharing this for parents to consider, but also for those who have had these experiences as a child to evaluate the effect and impact on your future and to provoke awareness of areas in your life to be healed and restored.

A Father Shapes Our Character

Fathers play a critical role in modeling behavior. They teach their children how to navigate the world, treat others respectfully, handle challenges gracefully, and express emotions healthily. Fathers must actively engage in their children's lives in today's fast-paced society to help shape their character.

For me, it was also my dad's practical side that has had a profound influence on my life. This practicality is a legacy passed down from his father, my grandad, who faced the immense challenges of farming during tough times. Growing up in an era marked by economic uncertainty and environmental hardships, my grandad learned to adapt and innovate out of sheer necessity. He taught my dad the importance of resilience and resourcefulness—qualities that have shaped our family's approach to life. I am sure those qualities helped my dad survive being a prisoner of war in World War Two when many around him did not!

This legacy of practical wisdom continues to guide me today. In a world often driven by fleeting trends and superficiality, I find strength in the lessons passed down through generations. It reminds me that success isn't just about ambition; it's about having the tenacity to face challenges head-on and making thoughtful decisions rooted in reality. My grandad's struggles on the farm may seem distant now, but their impact resonates deeply within our family—a testament to how practicality can be a powerful force for growth and stability in any life journey.

This heritage instilled in me a deep appreciation for hard work and ingenuity. My dad often shared stories of how his father would transform adversity into opportunity —whether it was repairing machinery with whatever materials were available or finding creative ways to stretch resources further than seemed possible. This mindset shaped not only their lives but also mine; it taught me that challenges are merely stepping stones toward growth and success.

Understanding this lineage of practicality has profoundly influenced how I approach obstacles in my own life. It encourages me to think critically about solutions rather than dwell on problems. Embracing a mindset that encourages critical thinking about solutions rather than fixating on problems can transform the way we approach challenges in our lives and work. When faced with obstacles, it's easy to get caught up in a cycle of negativity, analyzing what went wrong or lamenting the difficulties we encounter. However, shifting our focus to potential solutions empowers us to take action and fosters a proactive attitude.

This approach enhances our problem-solving skills, cultivates resilience, and avoids anxiety. By prioritizing solutions, we train ourselves to view setbacks as opportunities for growth. Rather than feeling defeated by challenges, we learn to dissect them critically, identify root causes, and brainstorm innovative ways to overcome them. God promises to work all things together for the good of those who love him. We see the possible positive result that the trial opens us up to instead of just the negativity we feel now.

Moreover, this solution-oriented mindset inspires collaboration and creativity within families and teammates at work or church. When everyone is encouraged to contribute ideas and think critically about how to address issues collectively, it leads to more diverse perspectives and more prosperous outcomes. Ultimately, by focusing on solutions instead of dwelling on problems, we improve our outlook and inspire those around us to adopt a similar perspective—creating an environment where progress thrives. Thus, a dad who faces the trials of life head-on and looks for solutions demonstrates an overcoming spirit to his wife and kids.

Our Log Truck Rolled Over

I remember when, as a young adult working with my dad on the farm and family sawmill, the news came back one day that our truck rolled over in the bush with a load of logs much needed for our orders to be fulfilled. I watched the look on my dad's face, which clearly showed the pressure of loss and what it would mean to our business. We were all feeling the same without much being said. After a short time, my dad looked up and said, "It will be ok, boys; it is a setback, but we will get up in the morning and find a way to get through this. We will just have to work a bit harder for a while, but we will get through this like we always do." We worked hard and got through.

My dad and grandad's legacy serves as a reminder that with determination and creativity, we can overcome

20

even the most daunting circumstances—and that is a lesson worth passing on to future generations.

As a boy, I was always amazed that Dad always had a way to build, make, or find a way to get the job at hand done. He made me feel that my dad could do almost anything, and nothing would stop him from finding a way through.

God is A Way Maker

As a son, I have embraced the profound quality of hope and trust instilled in me by my parents, and especially my dad. No matter the challenges we faced, there was always a belief that a way through existed—a guiding light in times of darkness.

This unwavering faith is not merely a family trait; it reflects the divine quality of life that Father God extends to each of us today, regardless of our past experiences. Consider this: God is not just a distant observer but actively engages in our lives as the 'God of the Breakthrough' and the 'Way Maker.' In moments when we feel lost or overwhelmed, He creates streams in our desert experiences —transforming barren places into sources of life and refreshment. When obstacles seem insurmountable, He paves a straight path through uncertainty, guiding us toward hope and renewal. He makes a straight way through the valleys and mountains of life.

21

In every valley where despair may linger, He provides clarity and direction. Each step taken with faith transforms those dark moments into opportunities for growth and restoration. When we allow Father God to lead us as a good dad, we discover that even the steepest climbs become manageable under His watchful care.

This truth can radically alter our perspectives. No matter where we've been or what we've faced, God's promise remains steadfast. His ability to break through barriers is not limited by our history; instead, it is enhanced by it. Our struggles become stepping stones for His miraculous works in our lives. By trusting in Him as the ultimate Way Maker, we open ourselves to possibilities beyond imagination—where healing occurs, dreams are realized, and futures are brightened. Let this unwavering faith inspire you to believe that no situation is too dire for God's transformative power; He stands ready to lead us into new beginnings filled with purpose and joy. It is like God stands outside your door and says, 'Behold, I stand at the door of your heart to partner with you for success and victory!' That's a Good Dad.!

In moments when life seems overwhelming, it's essential to remember that hope is available to everyone. It transcends our circumstances and provides a foundation for rebuilding and thriving. This promise of restoration and strength is woven into the fabric of our existence as children of God, inviting us to lean into it and embrace it.

Father God offers each of us a profound invitation today, one that transcends our past and illuminates our present. No matter the valleys we've traversed or the mountains we've faced, His promise remains steadfast: a straight path through life's complexities. This divine guidance is not contingent upon our past but is rooted in His unwavering love and grace.

Imagine standing at the foot of a daunting mountain, feeling overwhelmed by its sheer size and the weight of your past mistakes. Yet, in that moment, Father God extends His hand to guide you forward. He does not dwell on what has been but instead focuses on what can be —a journey filled with hope and purpose.

You can embrace this offer and let go of the burdens that weigh you down or let them keep you a prisoner of your past. Trust in Father God's ability to create a straight way through your life's challenges— because with Him by your side, no mountain is too high to conquer nor a valley too deep to navigate.

I am excited to share more about how this divine quality can manifest in our lives. Whether you've faced hardships or are simply seeking clarity amidst chaos, know that there is an abundance of hope waiting for you. Together, we will explore practical ways to embrace this gift and unlock the potential for transformation within ourselves.

Good Dad Bad Dad

CHAPTER TWO

Dads In The Bible

This discussion is not just for dads to learn from the Bible's Good Dads or Bad Dads; it's also crucial for their offspring to reflect on these paternal figures and understand how they shape their lives. Each story in the Bible offers valuable lessons that transcend generations, allowing children to recognize both positive and negative influences.

No parent is perfect—this truth resonates deeply in our human experience. However, by examining these biblical narratives, we can uncover profound insights into fatherhood and parenting that can help us reshape our perspectives. The stories of these fathers serve as a mirror, prompting us to evaluate our own relationships with our parents and how those dynamics have influenced our identities.

Ultimately, it's about transformation. By acknowledging the imperfections of parental figures, we empower ourselves to break cycles and foster healthier images of what it means to be a good parent or child. God is the only perfect model in this equation, guiding us toward understanding grace and redemption in every family relationship.

God the Father is the Perfect Role Model

God the Father stands as the ultimate benchmark for fatherhood in a world of imperfections. He embodies qualities that every father should aspire to, such as unconditional love, unwavering support, and boundless patience. While no human can reach the heights of His perfection, striving to emulate these divine traits can lead to profound growth and deeper connections within families.

Consider the way God offers guidance without judgment. He provides wisdom and direction while allowing His children the freedom to make their own choices. This balance of authority and compassion is something that earthly fathers can learn from—creating an environment where children feel safe to explore their identities while knowing they have a steadfast supporter in their corner.

Moreover, God's ability to forgive transcends any human understanding of grace. He teaches us that mistakes are part of life's journey and that His love

26

remains constant despite our shortcomings. By adopting this perspective, fathers can foster resilience in their children, encouraging them to learn from failures rather than fear them. I have always said that success is not from the absence of failure; it often is the ultimate result of failures with a desire to succeed.

Ultimately, looking towards God the Father as a role model enriches individual parenting styles and contributes positively to society. Embracing His example allows fathers everywhere to strive for excellence—one small step at a time—toward becoming better men and mentors for future generations.

Adam was the First Husband and Father

Parents play a crucial role in shaping their children's lives, and the Bible provides numerous examples of both good and bad parenting. By examining these stories, we can learn valuable lessons about the impact of parental influence on their offspring. Let's explore some compelling narratives that highlight this profound connection.

Throughout history, the thought of Adam as the first husband and father begins our understanding of Adam's role in these foundational roles of husband and father. As the first husband, Adam symbolizes the essence of partnership and companionship. Really, there was no one else but God.

The relationship between Adam and Eve was not merely about companionship; it was built on a foundation of shared goals and aspirations. They worked together in the Garden of Eden, demonstrating how collaboration can strengthen bonds and create a harmonious environment. However, their decision to disobey God introduced complexities that resonate through generations. There is a price to pay for disobedience.

Cause And Effect - Accountability

This pivotal moment emphasizes that mutual support is crucial but must be grounded in shared values and moral integrity. The consequences of their actions remind us that choices made within a relationship can have far-reaching effects, setting precedents for future generations. In today's world, couples can learn from Adam and Eve's story by prioritizing open communication and aligning on core Godly beliefs while navigating life's challenges together.

Ultimately, Adam and Eve highlight the delicate balance between support and accountability in marriage. Their legacy prompts us to reflect on how our decisions impact our relationship with God, marriage, and our offspring. Embracing this understanding of cause and effect can lead to healthier relationships built on trust, respect, shared responsibility, and accountability.

We can appreciate the timeless lessons by recognizing Adam's significance as a husband and father.

They had a sinless world, a perfect environment, and open communication with God, and they messed up badly. Christians today can still be led astray to disobey God and make a mess of things, but God provides a restoration plan through the gospel. The Bible calls Jesus the second Adam, who came as a result of Adam's disobedience to God, in obedience to God to redeem mankind back into a relationship with God.

King David and His Sons

The 'Sinful nature' that was ushered into the world through Adams's fall is seen in many Bible characters that fall prey to the enemy's schemes and temptations. Take, for instance, the story of King David and his son Absalom. David was a revered leader chosen and anointed by God, yet struggled in his role as a father. His failure to address Absalom's rebellion ultimately led to tragedy, demonstrating how neglect and lack of guidance due to distractions of work and responsibilities can have dire consequences. This story serves as a potent reminder that parents must actively engage with their children and instill values from an early age as a priority. It also shows the great love that King David had for his sons. When Absalom usurped his authority by winning the people's hearts and stole the kingdom from David, he chose to flee instead of fighting for his right to be king. It was as if David remembered that God had given him the Kingdom, so maybe God has chosen to give my son the kingdom?

This was not just confusion because it was his son, but it was his reverential fear of God that understood God puts kings in place and removes them. David demonstrated an understanding of respect for God's anointed through his experiences with King Saul. David was honored for the good and paid a price for the bad, but eventually was known as a man after 'God's Own Heart.' There is a lesson there if we take the time to think about it!

The Sins Of The Fathers Visit Down on the Children

The scriptures seem to indicate that David was not sure if God was pleased with him or not. David, as great a man and King, committed adultery and conspired to murder his lover's husband. His son Amnon raped his brothers daughter Tamar, and Absalom murdered his brother for this before waging the cue against his father. There is no doubt that outside of God's grace and forgiveness, a man will reap what a man sows. David seemed to clearly understand that it was God's right and privilege to be the judge and pass judgment.

David's story is one of remarkable triumphs and profound struggles. Anointed by God, he became a legendary figure known for his extraordinary feats— defeating a lion and a bear as a young shepherd and famously slaying Goliath with nothing but a sling and a stone. Yet, despite these monumental achievements, David faced significant challenges in his role as a father. His life was filled with responsibilities that often overshadowed the essential disciplines needed to nurture his children.

This paradox is not uncommon among busy fathers today. The demands of work, societal expectations, and personal ambitions can easily distract from the vital task of parenting. Just as David grappled with balancing his duties as king and father, many modern dads find themselves struggling to prioritize quality time with their kids amidst their hectic lives.

The consequences of neglecting this critical aspect of fatherhood can be profound. Children thrive on guidance, love, and discipline—elements that can easily slip through the cracks when parents are preoccupied with external pressures. David's legacy serves as a powerful reminder that even the most accomplished individuals must remain vigilant in their roles at home.

King David's parenting journey is a compelling story that encapsulates both triumphs and failures. As a father, he exhibited profound love and forgiveness towards his children, demonstrating the importance of compassion in family relationships. However, his struggles with discipline and accountability reveal a critical aspect of effective parenting that cannot be overlooked in his dealings with Absalom and Amnon.

As I mentioned, one of the most prominent examples of this struggle is in 2 Samuel 13, where we see David's failure to confront Amnon's egregious sin against Tamar, his brother Absalom's daughter. This pivotal moment not only illustrates David's inability to uphold justice within his family but also sets off a chain reaction of tragedy that reverberates through subsequent generations. By neglecting to address such serious wrongdoing, David inadvertently allowed resentment and discord to fester among his children.

Spare the Rod And You Will Spoil The Child

This weakness in David's approach serves as an important lesson for modern parents that love must be balanced with discipline. While it is essential to nurture our children with kindness and understanding, we must also instill values of accountability and justice. The consequences of overlooking these responsibilities can lead to devastating outcomes—just as they did in the house of David. In reflecting on King David's experiences, we are reminded that successful parenting requires both compassion and courage to confront difficult truths head-on.

These biblical accounts underscore an essential truth: Parents have an immense responsibility that extends beyond mere provision. They are tasked with molding character, instilling values, and providing direction. By reflecting on these stories, we gain insight into our parenting practices and recognize our lasting impact on our children's futures. We must strive to be mindful guardians who guide our offspring toward fulfilling lives rooted in integrity and purpose.

Ahab and Jezebel

Ahab and Jezebel are infamous for their wickedness and their negative influence on their children. Their sons, Ahaziah and Joram, followed in their evil ways, leading to disastrous consequences for their kingdom. 1 Kings 22:52 describes Ahab's legacy: "He did more to arouse the anger of the Lord, the God of Israel than did all the kings of Israel before him." It's not a good testimony before God, obviously! This serves as a cautionary tale of the destructive impact of parental corruption and disorder in the marriage relationship.

Role Reversal of Biblical Headship - Headship

The concept of biblical headship has long been a topic of discussion and debate within Christian households. The story of Jezebel and her manipulation of King Ahab to run the country through him, serves as a stark reminder of the dangers that arise when this divine order of male headship is reversed. Today, we witness a troubling trend in many families: traditional roles are flipped, leading to confusion and discord.

This role reversal often manifests in various ways: the wife takes on the primary leadership responsibilities, while the husband assumes a more passive role. Usually, with a passive husband, the wife assumes a more dominant role, sometimes overbearing and micromanaging the family. Most often she takes on the

33

role because the husband is not functioning and passively allows it.

While partnerships in marriage should be based on mutual respect and collaboration, it's crucial to recognize that God's design for headship is not merely about authority but about responsibility, guidance, and accountability. It is a spiritual positioning. When this structure is distorted, families can experience turmoil that impacts not just marital harmony but also the upbringing of children.

The Passive Husband

Often, when a wife plays the dominant role, it is because she was raised in a home where the mother was leading the family and the husband was passive or submissive for various reasons, like overworking or even alcohol problems. I am not inferring blame here but just giving examples that create disorder in the home. A passive husband often comes from a family where the dad is not the leader of the home. Again, I am not saying that they are evil like Ahab and Jezebel, but we are highlighting the reversal of roles exemplified in the extreme examples.

Biblical Headship

In 1 Corinthians 11:3, "... I want you to realize that the head of every man is Christ, and the head of the woman is man, and the head of Christ is God."This is

34

God's design and plan for the family. Ephesians describes the husband's role as head, loves his wife like Christ loved the church and laid down his life for her, and as a result, the wife respects and honors him. It is essential to say that without the power of God's love working in both, it may still lack the best result, but the foundation is set for success.

Positional Authority Releases God's Blessing

Embracing God's intended roles does not diminish equality; rather, it enhances the family dynamic by providing clarity and purpose. Husbands are called to lead with love and wisdom, while wives are encouraged to support their husbands in this journey with respect for what God honors. By restoring biblical headship in our homes, we can foster an environment where both partners thrive—each fulfilling their God-given roles while working together as good role models for their boys and girls. It's time for families to seriously consider these dynamics. By understanding and implementing God's design for headship, we can avoid the pitfalls seen throughout history—like those exemplified by Ahab and Jezebel—and create homes filled with peace, respect, and divine order.

Disclaimer - Ladies, Don't Get Angry

I know there are examples in homes where the husband is an addict, an abuser, or just plain useless for various reasons where the wife and mother has to rise to the occasion of leading the home. No judgment here, just emphasizing what God's best is for the family. If you know God's plan, maybe some can win him to his rightful position. It has been done!

Abraham Was A Good Dad

In the Old Testament, one of the most compelling examples of exemplary parenting and love of his family is found in the figure of Abraham. His relationship with his nephew Lot exemplifies not just kindness but a profound sense of responsibility and care that resonates deeply even today. When Abraham adopted Lot into his family, he did so with a heart full of compassion, treating him not merely as a servant or an obligation but as a beloved adopted son. Abraham became the Father of faith towards God, who chose to adopt us into his family. I believe much of Abraham's actions aided in opening the way for God to send his son to die for the sins world.

This nurturing bond is highlighted in Genesis 12:4, where Abraham's actions speak volumes about his character. He didn't just provide for Lot; he empowered him by allowing him to choose first from the land they were to inhabit. This act was not only generous but also indicative of Abraham's belief in giving others respect and right to choose, qualities that are essential for any good parent or guardian.

Abraham's approach to family dynamics teaches us invaluable lessons about love, sacrifice, and the importance of fostering strong relationships within our families. By prioritizing Lot's needs and desires over his own, Abraham set an example that underscores what it truly means to be a good parent and uncle—a legacy that continues to inspire us today. He treated Lot as a son before he had his own son. He pleased God with his actions and responses.

Faith Starts Out Weak And Becomes Strong

When it came time for Abraham to welcome his son, the narrative of faith took a pivotal turn. Despite God's promise of a miraculous heir, Abraham faltered in his faith journey. He allowed doubt to cloud his judgment, leading him to heed his wife Sarah's suggestions. In a moment of weakness, he chose to mate with their bondservant, Hagar, resulting in the birth of Ishmael.

This decision highlights a crucial point: even significant figures of faith can stumble as part of their faith journey. Abraham's love for Ishmael was undeniable; he cherished his firstborn son deeply. However, this act stemmed from a lack of trust in God's timing and plan.

The story powerfully reminds us that our human instincts and weakness often lead us astray when we fail to fully embrace divine guidance. It is also a warning not to try and make a prophetic promise come to pass and leave that up to God.

Ultimately, this chapter illustrates not only Abraham's shortcomings but also the complexity of faith itself. It's easy to become impatient and take matters into our own hands when faced with uncertainty. Yet true faith requires patience and reliance on God's promises—even when they seem delayed or impossible. This lesson resonates profoundly today as we navigate our journeys through doubt and desire to control our circumstances.

The Test of Faith And Love

The story of Abraham and Isaac challenges our understanding of faith, love, and obedience. When God commanded Abraham to sacrifice his beloved son, the narrative presents a profound dilemma: how does one reconcile deep love for a child with unwavering devotion to God? This moment is not merely about the act of sacrifice; it embodies the ultimate test of faith.

As Abraham prepares for this heartbreaking journey, we witness a man torn between two profound loves—his love for God and his love for his son. With a noticeable sadness in his heart, he tells Isaac they are going to make a sacrifice. This touching moment reveals the depths of Abraham's faith; he trusts in God's plan even when it seems incomprehensible.

This story serves as a potent reminder that true faith often requires us to confront our deepest fears and uncertainties. It challenges us to consider what we would be willing to give up in our own lives for the sake of our beliefs. The extreme test faced by Abraham invites us all to reflect on our journeys of faith—how far are we willing to go in demonstrating our love for God? In embracing this story, we find an opportunity to understand Abraham's struggle and examine our relationship with divine trust and unconditional love.

As much as I hope God would never ask us to do what he asked of Abraham, it was still a moment where Abraham had to trust that God loved Isaac as much or more than him. In Hebrews 11, the word says that Abraham believed that God could even raise his son from the dead to fulfill God's promise to bless the nations through his promised son. It is worth mentioning here that Abraham obviously grew strong in faith from the bond women to this moment. His ability to hear the voice of God and trust him was not overnight.

Romans 4:20-21 says, "Yet he did not waver through unbelief regarding the promise of God, but was strengthened in his faith and gave glory to God, being fully persuaded that God had power to do what he had promised." Abraham believed in God, and it was credited to him as righteousness, and he became the father of faith.

Father's love for his Son - My Own Experience

In 1996, we had our first of three major RV accidents, in which my son Daniel was severely hurt. His jaw and leg were broken badly, and he lost a lot of blood while pinned upside down in the wreck. As a father, I was heartbroken over the damage to my son on my watch. If God had asked if I would take my son's wounds and damage onto my body, I would have said yes, do it to me before God even finished the question. I would have rather the brokenness of my son to be upon me so my son could be spared the pain. I am sure Abraham would have felt the same, but he did not stagger in his faith.

It was some time after the accident that I was preaching on the Abraham Isaac sacrifice when I realized that I could not do what Abraham did, but that I now understood what it cost Father God to send his only begotten son Jesus to die as a sacrifice for us.

The Testing of Our Faith Has a Result

Many theologians would say when Abraham passed this final test of faith, God knew He could send His own son He loved for the sins of the people of the world because this human-created man could give up the son of his love in obedience to Him.

I have often wondered why it took so long for Abraham to receive his son of promise and why God asked Abraham to sacrifice Isaac when he was about 25 years old. Nearly fifty years have passed since when God promised Abraham a son. Now, Abraham was well over 125 years old when he was put to the final test of faith, which may have changed the world and eternity for us all. Did it take all that 125 years for Abraham to grow strong in Faith? We all begin with little faith, and if we walk with God through the trials of life, we have the opportunity, through the testing of our faith, to grow strong in faith. We

40

are all given 'the measure of faith,' the Bible says, but it is how we respond to god in the trials of our journey that mature our faith and spiritual life.

Good Dad Bad Dad

42

Good Dad Bad Dad

42

CHAPTER THREE

God's Balanced Home

God's desired Balanced Home is not merely a concept but a transformative vision for our lives and communities. At its core, this balance represents the harmony that God intends us to achieve in every aspect of our existence — spiritually, emotionally, and physically. Imagine a home where love reigns supreme and relationships flourish through understanding and compassion. This is the essence of God's desired Balanced Home.

In such an environment, individuals are encouraged to grow and thrive. Spiritual practices are integrated into daily life, fostering a deep connection with God while promoting inner peace. Emotional well-being is prioritized through open communication and support among family members, creating a safe space for vulnerability and healing. In my experience as a minister, this type of home is becoming more rare.

Moreover, physical balance plays a crucial role in this vision. By physical, I mean the active interaction of parents and children. A harmonious home promotes healthy living—not just through nutritious meals but also by nurturing an atmosphere filled with joy and creativity. This balance encourages everyone to pursue their passions.

Ultimately, striving for God's desired balanced home means embracing love, respect, and unity within our households. It invites us to reflect on how we can create environments that honor godly values—transforming our homes and potentially the world around us. Someone is always watching!

A Healthy Husband and Wife Relationship

The Bible offers profound insights into the relationship between husbands and wives, emphasizing the importance of love, respect, and partnership. Ephesians 5:25-33 shows a powerful directive for husbands to love their wives as Christ loved the church— sacrificially and unconditionally. This establishes a foundation of deep commitment that encourages couples to prioritize each other's well-being above their own. Christ laid down his life for the church, described as his bride. So, what does this mean in practice? Do husbands need to lay down their lives for their wives?

Laying Down Your Life For Your Wife

Years ago, when I was trying to understand this, I felt the Lord say to me, "Would you take a bullet for your wife?" I responded quickly with, "Absolutely I would." It was like he made me aware from that point that I was willing to take a bullet for my wife, but to pick up the wet towel and hang it up, or put my dirty clothes in the washing bin or put the coffee pot away…? It is incredible to me that, as men, we would take a bullet for our spouse but struggle with the thought of doing the little things that mean so much to our wife. The Bible says, "The small foxes spoil the vine." In other words, life's little things and moments spoil your relationship. Inversely, it can be what makes a relationship.

Think Like A Women

An older man once said to me, 'To have a successful marriage, there are many times you have to think like a woman.' At first, the manhood in me did not feel comfortable with what he was suggesting, but as time went by, I realized that women think differently about things than men. As a result, men constantly miss what their wives are saying to them and why. When you can take the time to think why your wife is harping on something that does not seem relevant to you, it just might mean the world to her for you to take it seriously.

Consider this: when your wife brings up an issue that may seem trivial or irrelevant to you, it's often more than a casual concern for her. It represents her feelings, her thoughts, and her need for connection. Understanding why she is continuously bringing it up can make all the difference in your relationship. You validate her emotions and strengthen your bond by showing genuine interest and empathy. When I finally got what this man was saying to me, a new aspect of my relationship with my wife began to open up. It is still hard sometimes for me not to react and bulldoze through with my thoughts, but when I take the time to listen and understand, some of the best decisions in our lives have been the result. The bottom line is that women can sometimes see what a man cannot see.

When put into practice, this discipline nurtures your relationship and sets an example for your children. The kids are always listening from somewhere. They learn what it means to communicate openly and support one another through life's challenges.

The love displayed between parents becomes a powerful blueprint for how they will approach their relationships in the future. Embracing these moments with care benefits you as a couple, and it's essential training for the next generation to cultivate lasting connections built on understanding and respect. When you stop and think about what you saw and heard from your parents and how it has shaped your life for better or worse, you should grasp what I am saying!

Women Are Fine Print And Men Are Headlines.

I remember coming home after a long day in the church office, listening to people's problems, running the church, sorting out staff problems, and walking through the door. My wife would ask me about my day, and my answer was often short, like "It was OK." She would push for details about how it went with so and so, and I would sum it up with "pretty good."

My wife was looking for details, and I just gave her the headlines. Women look for the fine print under the story's headline, while men are happy with the headline. The wife is genuinely interested in your day and how it went to make conversation after spending all day with the children and wishing you were here — at least in early marriage. Eventually, she will stop asking!

In reality, she probably wanted to open the conversation about your day so she could express how she felt about it and share her day with you. Eventually, she feels left out and misunderstood. The result of this lack of meaningful communication and empathy for each other leads to the beginning of a shutdown in the woman and the husband, puzzled, wondering what is wrong with her. Depending on who is reading this, you may see the pattern or be clueless about what is happening!

Subtle differences in communication can often be overlooked in relationships, leading to feelings of isolation and misunderstanding in both parties. When your wife seems fixated on an issue that appears trivial or irrelevant to you, it's crucial to pause and reflect on her perspective. This isn't merely a matter of annoyance; it signals that deeper emotions are at play.

When you take the time to consider why she is bringing up something that may seem insignificant from your point of view, you might uncover a profound need for validation and connection. If you approach the conversation with empathy and genuine interest, it could mean the world to her. Acknowledging her feelings, even if they don't resonate with your own experiences, fosters an environment where meaningful dialogue can flourish.

Ignoring these moments can lead to emotional shutdowns in women—a gradual withdrawal that leaves husbands puzzled about what went wrong. Instead of wondering why she has changed or what is troubling her, make it a priority to engage in open conversations where both partners feel heard and valued. This slight shift in approach strengthens your bond and enhances mutual understanding and compassion within your relationship.

In my experience, sometimes we end up where I thought we would, but with my wife's full support and understanding. In truth, we often end up in a better place that we both agree on and achieve together. This is a marriage of two people becoming one. You either become one, or you move towards emotional separation.

Emotional Separation

Most men don't realize what is happening until the gap is so vast that they come home to an empty house, and the wife and kids are gone. But the truth is that the wife left a long time before the physical separation. What is almost as bad is when the wife has left you but is still at home going through the motions.

A troubling pattern often emerges in many relationships: the gradual disconnection that can leave one partner feeling isolated and unheard. Most men don't realize what is happening until the gap has widened significantly. The emotional withdrawal starts subtly and progressively as a result of a lack of meaningful communication or empathy for each other's feelings but eventually reaches a breaking point.

What's almost as devastating is when a wife has emotionally left but remains physically present in the home, going through the motions of daily life. This scenario creates an environment filled with unspoken tension and confusion. The husband may wonder what went wrong, oblivious to his partner's silent struggle. But at least there is room for change. Both partners must recognize these signs early on—engaging in open dialogue and fostering genuine empathy can bridge this widening chasm before it becomes insurmountable. Understanding each other's emotional needs is vital; without it, couples risk losing their connection and family unit altogether!

The Two Shall Become One

The Bible's plan for the union of marriage:

"For this reason, a man shall leave his father and mother and be joined to his wife, the two shall become one flesh'; so then they are no longer two, but one flesh. Therefore what God has joined together, let not man separate."
Mark 10:7-8 NKJV

From God's perspective, the biblical union of marriage reveals a profound truth about connection and communication. However, when meaningful dialogue falters and empathy wanes, the consequences can be devastating.

When a woman feels left out and misunderstood in her marriage, it creates an emotional chasm that can lead to her shutting down. Her husband often misinterprets this withdrawal as disinterest or dissatisfaction in their relationship. He may wonder what has gone wrong or why his partner seems distant. Yet, at the heart of this disconnect lies a lack of intentional communication—a vital component that can nurture, create, and protect their bond with each other.

To prevent this cycle of emotional separation from taking root, both partners must foster an environment where open dialogue thrives. The word '*Foster*' here means to encourage, promote, stimulate, and develop the environment.

It's essential for husbands as the '*head of the home*' to recognize the signs of emotional withdrawal and approach their wives with compassion rather than anger or confusion. By prioritizing empathy and understanding each other's feelings, especially during challenging times, they can strengthen their connection and fulfill the divine purpose of becoming "one flesh."

God's divine blueprint for marriage is beautifully expressed in the scripture, *"For this reason a man shall leave his father and mother and be joined to his wife, the two shall become one flesh; so then they are no longer two, but one flesh. Therefore what God has joined together, let not man separate."* This profound truth highlights the sacred union intended for husbands and wives, a partnership where both individuals think, act, and feel as one in the vital areas of their lives.

Achieving this unity may seem rare in many marriages today, but God's help and intervention make it possible. Inviting Him into your relationship allows you to cultivate an environment where love flourishes and differences are harmonized. Fostering this oneness takes intentional effort by aligning their hearts and minds through prayer, open communication, and mutual respect grounded in faith.

When partners commit to becoming 'one,' they embrace a journey that transforms their marriage into a powerful testimony of God's love. This unity strengthens their bond and serves as an example to others of how divine support can lead to lasting fulfillment. Remember that with God at the center of your relationship, there is nothing too challenging to overcome; together, you can achieve the beautiful oneness that He intends for every husband and wife.

Biblical Headship in the Home

In our first year of marriage, I struggled with Karen, who wanted me to clean up and put everything away when I made the coffee. My answer would be, "We will probably have another one later, and then I will clean up." She was not happy! I remember thinking when a man works in the shed and cuts a piece of timber, he does not clean up after every cut...! Eventually, the take the bullet story got through, and I began to lay down my life for my wife in the little things. It is little to me but so significant to my wife. As a result, I earned the respect of my wife.

In Ephesians 5:22-24, The instruction to wives continues. Wives are called to respect their husbands. Now, the two thoughts of Scripture make perfect sense. As the husband lays down his life for his wife, she is loved eventually to a place of respect, and love submission is the result. As they submit to one another in reverence for Christ and his word, love is made complete in the marriage. This mutual submission fosters an environment of trust and cooperation where both partners feel valued and heard. This affects the children positively and creates a healthy atmosphere for the family to prosper.

The biblical model encourages couples to work together as a team, reflecting a relationship built on equality and shared purpose yet understanding that the man is the head of the home when a man understands his role as head of the home and loves his wife and family as Christ loved the church and laid his life down, blessing results in every area.

Unfortunately, a lot of men take these same scriptures out of context and demand their wives submit to them instead of understanding the part about laying down your life first. Jesus first loved us and laid his life down for us so we could respond out of love and respect for his sacrifice for us.

Moreover, 1 Corinthians 13:4-7 outlines the characteristics of love that should define every marriage— patience, kindness, humility, and perseverance. By embodying these qualities within their relationship, husbands and wives can cultivate a strong bond that withstands life's challenges.

The Bible teaches that a successful husband-wife relationship is rooted in mutual love and respect. This foundational principle is not merely a suggestion; it's a divine blueprint for building strong marriages that can withstand life's challenges. When couples embrace these scriptural teachings, they cultivate an environment where both partners feel valued and cherished.

As described in 1 Corinthians 13:4-8, love transcends mere affection; it embodies patience, kindness, and selflessness.

"Love is patient, love is kind. It does not envy, it does not boast, it is not proud. It does not dishonor others; it is not self-seeking; it is not easily angered, and it keeps no record of wrongs. Love does not delight in evil but rejoices with the truth. It always protects, always trusts, always hopes, always perseveres. Love never fails."

Respect is born in a healthy marriage, which fosters open communication. Understanding these principles creates a harmonious partnership that honors each other and sets a powerful example for children.

By modeling love and respect in their interactions, couples demonstrate to their children the values of healthy relationships. Children learn from what they observe — when they see their parents treating each other with dignity and care, they internalize these behaviors as essential components of any relationship. Thus, embracing biblical principles isn't just about enhancing the marital bond; it's about protecting the next generation by instilling in them the importance of love and respect in all their future relationships. Needless to say, this as a reality.... is missing in most homes.

CHAPTER FOUR

Meaningful Communication

I have discussed the importance of communication several times, including meaningful dialogue in marriage and family relationships, sharing our hurts and burdens, etc.

Meaningful dialogue is the bridge that connects us in our most intimate relationships, whether in marriage or within our families. We can share our hurts and burdens through open communication, fostering more profound understanding and healing. Many relationships and marriages are destroyed because of poor communication or an inability to express what you are feeling or what is bothering you.

In hindsight, I realize that the real reason for my silence in areas of my past life was not just a desire for privacy but rather the weight of hurt and strongholds that kept painful experiences locked away. For years, they can hold you captive as a prisoner of your past.

By finally opening up about things of the past, you will discover the transformative power of this meaningful dialogue, allowing you to break free from the chains of your past. It's time we embrace vulnerability as a strength and recognize that true healing begins with honest conversations about what has shaped us. Again, I stress opening up only to a trusted, experienced person who understands God's ways and His healing.

Unspoken thoughts can be heavy, often leading to feelings of isolation and despair. However, by articulating these emotions, we allow ourselves to confront them head-on. David faced the Lion and the bear head-on, preparing to take on the giant who was boasting and mocking him.

By finally opening up about things of the past, you will discover the transformative power of this meaningful dialogue, allowing you to break free from the chains of your past through the power of the Holy Spirit. It's time we embrace vulnerability as a strength and recognize that true healing begins with honest conversations about what has hurt or is hurting you.

My Experience of Being a Poor Listener

Communication is a two-way street. Sharing and listening are vital to good communication in any relationship. Reflecting on my journey, I came to the Lord with a broken heart after my first wife left me—an experience that struck me like lightning in a blue sky. It took time for me to understand that I had not fully listened to her. I was caught up in my feelings and did not hear her concerns or needs.

This realization was pivotal. It taught me that meaningful dialogue requires both parties to engage openly and honestly. When we share our stories and actively listen, we create space for understanding and healing that could avoid brokenness and divorce.

One day, after the breakup, we had an opportunity to talk, and I said I struggled to understand what I had done wrong to cause her to leave me. This story she told me changed my understanding and is a major contributor to my successful marriage today with Karen.

My Ex-wife said that when I went to work, she would often sit under the lemon tree in our backyard and cry because I would not hear what she was saying to me.

The Bible says there are none so blind as those who will not see. Well, there are none who are so deaf that they will not hear either! I am unsure why I could not hear what she was trying to tell me, but I feel I was listening

57

through filters of my selfishness and pride, which canceled out what she was saying. Sometimes, you think or assume you are listening but you are just waiting to say what you want to say and not taking in what is being said.

In those days, I was so caught up in working hard from daylight to dark in the family saw-milling business, and I just thought she would know I loved her by working 16 hours a day. In reality, I just had no real clue what love was. My intentions were good, and I was a hard worker, but I was ignorant of my girl's needs. What was I thinking? I took a city girl down to my farm life in the middle of what must have felt like the middle of nowhere. The nearest neighbor was a mile away. I thought she would be happy living there, milking the house cow in the morning, feeding the chickens, collecting the eggs, and tending the vegetable garden while I was earning the money. Because I loved this lifestyle, I could not hear her cry of loneliness or despair until it was too late.

For years, as I pressed into God, I often shed tears imagining the love of my then life, crying under that lemon tree in the backyard. This powerful image became a powerful metaphor in my ministry, which I shared repeatedly with husbands on the brink of losing their wives. Husbands on the brink of losing their wives often find themselves grappling with confusion and despair when their wife starts to become withdrawn. They can often make it worse by getting irritable or overbearing because they feel rejected. And now the gap of mutual understanding gets wider and wider. Understanding that a woman's needs extend far beyond the traditional example of a hard-working man who offers surface-level acknowledgment of love is crucial. What she truly craves is a deep emotional connection and unwavering support.

Good communication in any relationship hinges on understanding one another deeply, not just hearing words but grasping the emotions behind them. If you find yourself at this crossroads, take this as an opportunity for growth. Invest time in fostering open dialogue with your wife. Ask questions, listen actively, and validate her feelings. The path may be challenging, but rebuilding that emotional bridge will be worth every effort you make.

Husbands on the brink of losing their wives, either physically or emotionally, often find themselves at a crossroads, unsure of how to bridge the emotional gap that has developed over time. As highlighted in 1 Peter 3:7, *"Husbands, in the same way, be considerate as you live with your wives, and treat them with respect as the weaker partner and as heirs with you of the gracious gift of life, so that nothing will hinder your prayers."* This scripture underscores the importance of deep emotional connection and mutual respect within marriage.

A surface-level acknowledgment of love won't suffice; women crave understanding, compassion, and genuine support from their husbands. They yearn for conversations that delve into their feelings and experiences rather than just sharing daily logistics or accomplishments. By fostering an environment where vulnerability is welcomed and emotions are honored, husbands can create a bond that strengthens their relationship and enriches both partners' lives.

Stepping Outside the Comfort Zone For Your Wife

My note to husbands: It's time to shift our focus from merely being providers with benefits to becoming partners who actively nurture their wives' emotional well-being.

Many men may find this concept foreign, as society often forces us to believe that hard work and financial stability are the cornerstones of a successful marriage. However, the truth is that your wife craves more love, a deep emotional connection, and a feeling of being understood.

This transition requires a significant mindset shift and, frankly, a lot of dying to self. It involves stepping outside your comfort zone, learning to listen actively, and understanding her feelings without judgment. It means prioritizing quality time and genuine interest in her thoughts and dreams. By investing in this emotional bond, you not only strengthen your relationship but also create an environment where both partners can thrive.

Don't wait until it's too late—embrace this challenge now. The rewards will be immeasurable: a happier wife, a more fulfilling partnership, and a more profound love that withstands the test of time. When men take this step toward a more profound connection, they enhance their marriage and lay a foundation for lasting love and harmony. You know how the saying goes…..' Happy Wife, Happy Life."

Good Dad Bad Dad

CHAPTER FIVE

Media And Children

In today's society, we must advocate for more responsible practices in what our children see and hear on Media platforms that glamorize harmful ways and habits. It's our duty as parents to create an environment where kids can learn positive behaviors instead of imitating negative ones seen on screen or heard in music.

Media Becomes The Baby Sitter

In today's digital age, the media begins to influence our children from infancy, often before they can even comprehend what they are watching. While it may be tempting for parents to hand over a smartphone or tablet for a moment of peace, this convenience comes with significant consequences. Allowing unrestricted access to screens creates a false virtual world that can distort their understanding of reality.

Children are impressionable, and when they consume content designed for adults or unrealistic portrayals of life, it fosters an increased desire to seek out more. This constant exposure can lead to unrealistic expectations and a skewed perception of the world around them. Instead of nurturing curiosity and creativity through real-world experiences, we risk cultivating an insatiable appetite for digital stimuli that may hinder their emotional and social development.

As responsible caregivers, we must reconsider how we introduce media into our children's lives. Setting boundaries on screen time and curating age-appropriate content can help ensure that our children grow up grounded in reality rather than lost in a virtual fantasy. It is crucial to engage with them in meaningful ways that foster genuine connections and encourage exploration beyond the screen.

Media starts to parent our children from infancy when many parents allow their children to watch various things on their smartphones or tablets. I understand the convenience of this practice, but it can create a false virtual world for the children and foster an increased desire to see and search out what is not healthy for them.

In today's digital age, it's undeniable that kids today are spending significantly more time glued to screens than engaging in outdoor play like my generation did. This shift is not just a passing trend; it's a cultural transformation that warrants our attention.

Research indicates that children now average over seven hours of screen time daily, which starkly contrasts with the active lifestyles enjoyed by kids in the past. Back then, playing outside was the norm—climbing trees, riding bikes, and exploring nature were integral parts of childhood. These activities fostered not only physical health but also social skills and creativity.

Effects Of Too Much Screen Time

The implications of this screen-centric lifestyle are profound. While technology offers educational benefits and connectivity, it also contributes to rising rates of obesity and mental health issues among children. The lack of physical activity can lead to long-term health consequences, while excessive screen time can hinder their ability to engage meaningfully with peers.

Parents and educators should prioritize encouraging outdoor play. By creating environments where children can thrive away from screens—through organized sports, community events, or family outings—we can help them rediscover the joys of nature and physical activity.

The Effects of Out Door Activities.

Recently my grandchildren visited our farm. One day, I returned from my farm work and realized they were sitting inside watching TV on a beautiful day. I interrupted and asked how would you like to ride on the four-wheelers down to the creek. They responded well, and off we went to the creek. They investigated every trail and waterhole for the next three or four hours and collected smooth rocks. They asked if they could build a bridge with rocks across the creek, and they worked together with fantastic energy and creativity to build that crossing. They loved it and wanted to do more. We rode horses, collected eggs, and fed the cows, the horses, and the ducks. My wife bought them some farm boots, and every morning, they would get up to go feed the chickens and collect the eggs.

Growing up on a farm, I was involved in outdoor chores that shaped not only my work ethic but also my appreciation for nature and family bonding. Every day spent alongside my dad and brothers taught me the value of hard work, responsibility, and the simple joys of life. Whether feeding the animals or tending to the crops, each task became an opportunity for laughter and learning.

Learning the Satisfaction of Finishing a Job

One of the most valuable learning experiences from my dad was not only to work hard but also to experience deep satisfaction when the job was done. Not every job was fun, and some were downright horrible, but no matter what the job was, the immense satisfaction of getting it done made it all worthwhile. Personally, that trait, taught to me by my dad, has got me through some of the most challenging times and projects in my life. It is a trait not to give up just because the going gets difficult or uncomfortable. Many young people today do not want to work; when they do, they often give up and look for something easier.

Get Outside kids

Fast-forward to today, and I am thrilled to see that my grandchildren share my enthusiasm for outdoor chores. When given the chance to step away from screens and immerse themselves in nature, they light up with excitement. This is a reminder that these experiences are timeless; they foster connection not just with our surroundings but also with one another. Encouraging kids to engage in outdoor tasks instills a sense of accomplishment and nurtures their curiosity about the world around them.

Let's not underestimate the power of these simple activities. I realize that not everyone has access to a farm lifestyle, but outdoor activities are available if they choose to look. By allowing children to participate in outdoor chores, we are giving them a gift—a chance to learn valuable life skills while creating cherished memories that will last a lifetime. It's clear that when given the opportunity, kids thrive outdoors, just as we did years ago on our family farm.

What Activity Was the Most Important in a Family?

When I was a young adult, I often found myself invited to the home of what seemed like the perfect family in our church. They had a great mum and dad, along with amazing kids who always appeared genuinely happy together. Curiosity got the better of me one day, and I asked the dad what their secret to such happiness and strong bonding was. To my surprise, the father replied simply: "Camping as a family."

I was intrigued and pressed him for more details. "Why camping?" I asked. "What made it so special?" He explained that camping provided them with an opportunity to disconnect from their busy lives and reconnect with each other, away from all the interruptions. Away from screens and distractions, they shared stories around the campfire, hiked through beautiful landscapes, and engaged in team-building activities like setting up tents, collecting firewood, or cooking meals together. These experiences fostered communication, teamwork, and cherished memories, strengthening their family bond.

The simplicity of camping allowed them to appreciate each other's company without everyday pressures weighing them down. It became a tradition that not only created lasting memories but also taught valuable life skills—resilience in facing challenges outdoors and gratitude for the little things in life.

The dad continues to share that it was terrific how unforgettable stories would be told around the family dinner table of the great times they had camped. I never forgot this discussion.

My experience going Bush with my Kids.

Years ago, when our children were small, I was burdened down with the church we were pastoring. My family was offered a stay in the mountains on an old farm property. I talked my wife and kids into going on a vacation so my kids could experience a time like my childhood on a farm.

We arrived at this somewhat run-down old farmhouse, and I noticed my wife and kids frown as we unpacked. I was excited because it felt just like my grandparents' old farmhouse, with creaky floorboards and a big verandah. The old kitchen had a wood-burning stove, just like the one I would use to cook toast on a long fork in the mornings as a kid.

How Long Are We Here Dad

My family could not see the place the same way I did. We had always gravitated towards beach houses or resort-style accommodations, where modern conveniences were a given. Their initial hesitation was pretty obvious when I suggested a more rustic getaway. The first day was indeed challenging. They missed the comforts of home and struggled to adjust to a simpler lifestyle. They asked, " How long do we have to stay here, Dad? "

However, as the days unfolded, something remarkable happened. We began to bond over shared experiences—hiking through trails, cooking meals together with ingredients sourced from what we shot, food found in local markets, and stargazing without the interference of city lights. Learning to watch out for snakes and spiders and know how to be safe in the bush. Slowly but surely, my family started to embrace this new way of experiencing our time together.

By the end of our trip, their perspectives shifted dramatically. They realized that sometimes stepping outside of our comfort zones can lead to unforgettable memories and deeper connections. What began as reluctance transformed into enthusiasm for future adventures in places that offered more than just luxury— they found joy in simplicity and authenticity instead.

This experience taught us that it's not about where you stay but how you engage with each other and your surroundings that genuinely matters. Little did we know that this was just an introduction to the rest of our lives as a family traveling around the world together. Now, we have more stories 'than you could poke a stick at'… as we would say in Australia!

So next time you're looking for ways to enhance your family's connection or create lasting memories together, consider taking a break from your routine and heading out into nature. You might just discover that the secret isn't just about camping; it's about making time for each other amidst life's chaos.

Today's youth needs to experience the rich tapestry of life outside their screens; after all, those moments spent outdoors are foundational in shaping well-rounded individuals who will thrive in an increasingly digital world.

Good Dad Bad Dad

CHAPTER SIX

A Fatherless Generation

W e have often heard the statement, "This is a fatherless generation.... As discussed earlier, this is not always because the father is not physically present but because the role model is missing.

A lot of this younger generation is missing the biblical morals that the Word of God encourages, with a decline in the family unit. The assertion that we are witnessing a fatherless generation resonates deeply in today's society. However, it's crucial to recognize that this absence is not solely about the physical presence of fathers; it often stems from a lack of role models and guidance. Many young individuals grow up without the foundational biblical morals that have historically shaped family structures and societal values.

73

Impact on Our Youth

When we discuss the decline of family dynamics, we must consider how the absence of strong moral frameworks impacts our youth. Scripture offers invaluable lessons on love, respect, and responsibility—essential for nurturing healthy relationships and building resilient families. Without these guiding principles, many young people find themselves adrift, struggling to establish their identities and navigate the complexities of life.

Increase of Single Mothers

I believe this lack of understanding in society as a whole has led to many young girls becoming pregnant and becoming single mothers, thus, no male role model for the children in the home. Broken homes often lead to the same problems, with stepfathers not always being good dads to the kids.

I believe this lack of understanding in society has led to a troubling cycle that affects not only young girls but also the future generations they raise. When young girls find themselves unprepared for the responsibilities of motherhood, the consequences can be profound.

Identity Crisis in Young People

The many who become single mothers, navigating life without a male role model for their children, can create an environment where boys may struggle to understand what it means to be a man and where girls may lack guidance on healthy relationships.

Gender Confusion

This has given birth to gender confusion throughout the younger generation. When mothers raise children without a male role model, it can lead to significant gaps in understanding gender roles and healthy relationships. Boys may find themselves grappling with what it means to be a man, lacking the guidance that typically comes from having a strong father figure. This absence can foster confusion about masculinity, leaving them unsure of how to express their identity or engage in relationships.

Similarly, girls raised in these environments may struggle to clearly understand healthy interactions with men. Without positive male influences, they might inadvertently adopt unhealthy relationship patterns or develop unrealistic expectations about love and partnership. This dynamic not only affects individual families but also contributes to broader societal issues, including gender confusion and miscommunication between genders.

It's essential to recognize the importance of role models—whether through mentorship programs or church community involvement, to help bridge these gaps. By fostering environments where both boys and girls can learn about respect, empathy, and healthy relationships from various sources, we can combat the confusion that arises from the absence of traditional family structures. In doing so, we empower future generations with the tools they need for personal growth and meaningful connections.

Broken homes often perpetuate these issues. Step-fathers do not always step into their roles with the commitment and care needed to foster a nurturing environment. In some cases, they may contribute further to instability rather than providing the support that children desperately need. The result is a cycle of emotional and social challenges that can follow children into adulthood, affecting their ability to form stable relationships and raise their own families.

Society must address these gaps in understanding and support systems. By addressing open discussion about relationships, parenting, and parent responsibility, we can work towards breaking this cycle and ensuring that more children have access to positive role models—both male and female—in their lives.

Back To Biblical Morals

As we reflect on this pressing issue, it becomes evident that fostering an environment where biblical morals are brought back into our education system. It is often the opposite these days in the schooling system. If we can find a way to access this instruction, we can significantly counteract this trend in our lives and the lives of others. We can help instill these vital values in the younger generation by encouraging mentorship and positive role modeling within our communities. It is imperative to take action now.

Good Dad Bad Dad

CHAPTER SEVEN

A Father To The Fatherless

In a world where so many face the pain of abandonment and loss, the promise that God's word offers to be a 'Father to the Fatherless' is not just comforting—it's transformative. This divine assurance speaks directly to those who feel isolated, neglected, or abandoned, reminding us that we are never truly alone.

Absentee Fathers

I have realized that a father does not have to die to be absent in a child's life. The dad can still be at home and be absent in a child's life. It can be his personality, addiction to alcohol, addiction to work, or a successful dad who loves his kids with money instead of being present in their lives.

The truth is that a father's physical presence does not guarantee emotional availability. Many children grow up with fathers who are physically at home yet emotionally miles away. This absence can stem from various factors: an overwhelming addiction to work that prioritizes career over connection, an unhealthy reliance on alcohol that clouds judgment and engagement, or even a relentless pursuit of success that leaves little room for nurturing relationships.

As a boy, I had a friend whose dad was a Doctor and lived in a big home with all the things money could buy. My dad worked hard and had a farm and a small house in Sydney, Australia, that was very small compared to my friend's sprawling estate. I must admit I was often embarrassed when my friend came to our home.

One time, my friend came down to our farm for a holiday. Our old family farmhouse was awesome in hindsight, but it had no electricity, kerosine lamps, a kerosine fridge, and a wood-burning stove. At the end of these school holidays, a simple statement from my friend shifted my entire perspective on my relationship with my dad. With tears glistening in his eyes, he turned to me and said, "Doug, I wish your dad was my dad."

At that moment, I realized how much I took for granted. While many of us often equate happiness with material possessions or status, it became clear that the love and support of a parent are invaluable treasures that money simply cannot buy. My friend saw a relationship

80

with my dad that he just did not have with all their wealth. We chopped wood, rode horses, went shooting in the mornings, and spot-lighting for rabbits at night. We sat by the open fire at night, sharing stories with my dad. It was usual for me but not for my wealthy friend.

My friend's heartfelt admission made me appreciate the moments spent with my dad—those seemingly mundane afternoons filled with laughter, lessons learned during our long talks about life while we worked on farm projects, and his unwavering belief in me. It dawned on me that these experiences shaped who I am far more than any expensive gift ever could. This realization prompted me to reflect on what truly matters in life: relationships built on love and trust with my dad were 'priceless,' but everything else of less value can be bought with an Amex card.

Real Relationships Priceless

As we navigate life's challenges and successes, we must remember to cherish those connections that bring us joy and comfort. My friend's words served as a potent reminder that while wealth can provide temporary satisfaction, the bonds we forge with our loved ones—like my bond with my dad—create lasting fulfillment. By embracing this truth, I not only enriched my own life but also inspired me to ultimately touch other lives.

At the time, I was somewhat stunned by his statement, but it opened my eyes to what wealth was! This has had a profound and lasting effect on my life as a son, a father, and a minister, to value what money cannot buy.

The bond suffers when a father equates love with financial support rather than quality time and genuine interactions. Children need their fathers to be present—not just in body but in spirit and mind. All children naturally crave attention, affection, and guidance that cannot be replaced by material gifts. The impact of this emotional absence can be profound, leading to feelings of neglect and confusion about love, and can often be replaced with pride in life and position.

Fathers must recognize the importance of involvement in their children's lives. Building memories through shared experiences fosters stronger relationships than any amount of money ever could. A father's role should extend beyond providing for the family. It should encompass being there—listening, engaging, and participating in the everyday moments that shape a child's development as much as possible. After all, actual presence is about more than just being home; it's about being truly there for your child when they need you most.

God is a present Father.

God's commitment to care for the vulnerable is woven throughout scripture, providing hope and strength where it is most needed. From Psalm 68:5, which describes God as "a father to the fatherless," to James 1:27, which emphasizes pure religion as caring for orphans and widows, we see a clear message: God sees our struggles and actively seeks to support us.

"A father of the fatherless, a defender of widows,
Is God in His holy habitation.
God sets the solitary in families;
He brings out those who are bound into prosperity;
But the rebellious dwell in a dry land." Psalm 68:5-6

These scriptures reveal profound truths about God's character and His unwavering commitment to caring for the vulnerable. "A father of the fatherless, a defender of widows," these verses reveal God's role as a protector and provider, emphasizing His divine presence and purpose in our lives.

The promise that "God sets the solitary in families" speaks to our innate need for community and belonging. It reassures us that no one is truly alone, as God actively works to bring people together, fostering relationships that nurture and uplift.

Many who have been lonely have found great comfort in a good, healthy church family, especially if they have come from a dysfunctional family household. Moreover, the declaration that He "brings out those who are bound into prosperity" offers hope for those feeling trapped by their circumstances. These truths, when realized, encourage believers to trust in God's plan even when faced with adversity.

In contrast, the warning that "the rebellious dwell in a dry land" reminds us of the consequences of straying from God's guidance. It invites us to reflect on our choices and consider how aligning with God's will leads to fulfillment rather than desolation and isolation.

It encourages us to delve deeper into the promises in His word to find clarity and conviction, allowing His teachings to transform our hearts and minds. This promise of Father God's desire to look after and protect us goes beyond mere words; it invites us into a relationship characterized by love, guidance, and protection. This assurance can instill a sense of belonging and purpose in those who have experienced loss or lack. It encourages individuals not only to seek trust and comfort in their faith but also inspires them to extend that same compassion toward others in need. Jesus said, "Love one another with the love you are experiencing from Him."

Embracing this truth keeps us moving toward healing in our lives, reminding us that even in our darkest moments, there is an unwavering light ready to guide us home. Whether you are seeking comfort for yourself or looking for ways to support others who may feel lost or abandoned, remember that God's promise stands firm: He will always be a Father to the fatherless.

Here are some Bible verses about parenting:

Proverbs 22:6: *"Start children off on the way they should go, and even when they are old, they will not turn from it."*

Ephesians 6:4: *"Fathers, do not provoke your children to anger by the way you treat them. Rather, bring them up with the discipline and instruction that comes from the Lord".*

Remember, "It's Only Theory Until You Do It" is the title of Doug's book that Touches deeper on walking in the Spirit of God's ways and promises.

Good Dad Bad Dad

CHAPTER EIGHT

Father-Figure to the Fatherless

If a family does not have a dad at home, such as a single mother or a dad who has died, the mother needs to seek a father figure who will be involved in the children's lives. A trusted, strong male influence can help balance a family with an absent father.

The importance of seeking a father figure cannot be overstated in families without a father. A strong male presence can provide children with essential guidance, support, and stability during their formative years. It's not just about filling a void; it's about creating a balanced environment where children can thrive emotionally and socially.

A father figure can offer different perspectives and life lessons crucial for development. This male presence becomes invaluable through mentorship, participation in family activities, or simply being there to listen and advise. It helps foster resilience and balance in children by providing them with a role model who embodies strength, responsibility, and compassion, which is missing when children do not have a dad.

This role model could be an uncle, family friend, grandfather, or a possible new husband for the wife. If he is the possible new husband, it is vital that he loves and is respected by the children if he takes on the role of the kid's dad or stepdad. I have heard tragic story after story of new men in the lives of the kids who have caused severe detriment to the boys and girls of a broken family.

In Comes the Stepdad

When a mother is contemplating introducing a new man into the family dynamic, remarkably if he is poised to take on the role of husband or father figure, it becomes imperative that this individual embodies love and respect, not only for the mother but also for her children.

There is tragic story after tragic story about new men entering these families, leaving behind trails of emotional turmoil and damage. These experiences highlight the importance of ensuring that any potential stepfather or father figure fosters a nurturing environment where children feel safe and cherished.

If this new man is to assume such an essential role in their lives, he must genuinely connect with the children, building trust and respect rather than merely fulfilling obligations. The stakes are high, and failing to prioritize these relationships can lead to severe detriment for both boys and girls in broken families.

Therefore, it's vital for husbands who have taken on this role with someone else's children to recognize that true love encompasses not just partnership but also an understanding of how family bonds should be nurtured with care and compassion.

So whether you are the biological father, the new man in the family, or a mom seeking a new husband, you must understand that a father figure can significantly impact children's self-esteem and confidence for their future. They learn what healthy relationships look like through positive interactions with this individual. This connection is especially vital for young boys who benefit from seeing how men should behave—respectfully towards others and themselves—and young girls who gain insights into how they should be treated in relationships.

Ultimately, seeking out a good father figure isn't just beneficial; it's essential for nurturing well-rounded individuals who understand the value of masculine and feminine influences. Making this effort can lead to profound changes that resonate throughout their lives long after childhood has passed. I have witnessed both good and bad dads in families and ministered to them over many years. When a good dad role is in place in the family, the best results are secure, but all too many times,

I have been part of a sad story of abuse when a bad dad ends up on the scene.

There Is Healing For ALL

Suppose you identify with any of these scenarios as a mother, dad, stepdad, or child of a dysfunctional family, my message beyond the sad reality of confusion and strife is that there is freedom, healing, and change for all the affected persons with the help of God. Without a godly intervention, the results of most lives continue to be sad and damaging.

Gender Confusion Becoming More Common

As mentioned earlier, my desire is for a positive change in children from a balanced parental influence, but I am concerned about the confusion over gender in recent times. Boys wanting to be girls and girls wanting to be boys is mainly due to the parental imbalance in society today.

Recently, we have witnessed a growing conversation about gender identity, particularly among children. While I desire a positive change that fosters understanding and acceptance, I cannot help but express my concerns about the confusion surrounding gender roles in today's society. An increasing number of boys seem to desire to be girls and vice versa, which raises important questions about the influences shaping these identities.

In my discussion with kids caught up in this confusion, it is common for them to say they believe they were born this way with these urges to be gay or to be the opposite sex. I empathize with anyone who truly believes something, but that belief is birthed for many reasons.

Parental balance—or the lack thereof- is at the heart of this issue. Much because we truly are living in a fatherless generation.'Many families today face challenges that disrupt traditional structures and lead to imbalances in parenting styles. This can create an environment where children may feel uncertain about their identities or roles within society. When parents are not aligned in their values or approaches to child-rearing, it can leave children feeling confused and seeking clarity in ways that may not always be healthy.

Parents must establish a balanced approach that provides stability and guidance while allowing children to explore their identities safely. Open conversations about gender should be encouraged within supportive frameworks rather than leaving kids to navigate these complex feelings alone or influenced by external pressures that seem to be in the education system, unfortunately. If we educate children to think that they can choose what gender they are according to their feelings and impressions, it permits them to do just that.

As we strive for progress and inclusivity, we also recognize the importance of nurturing environments where children can develop their sense of self without confusion stemming from parental imbalance or non-parental influence in the education system. Only then can we hope for a future where all individuals feel secure in who they are, regardless of gender, while being grounded in supportive family relationships that nurture their God-given identity.

These are only some contributing factors, but they are major contributors. If you have a balanced parental influence in the home, with a dad who is the head of the home and keeps order with love and devotion, the kids have the best chance of maturing without hangups that rob their lives.

There Is An Answer

As I said, no matter what past circumstances caused problems in a person's life, an intimate relationship with God has been the main reason I have seen many folks find healing and restoration from the confusing situations that are becoming all too common in many families.

In the journey of healing and personal growth in a male or female, the influence of a positive male figure can be transformative, especially for young individuals who have faced the absence of a father or endured abuse. I have often encouraged young men and women to seek out a father figure actively. This isn't about replacing their biological father; it's about enriching their emotional landscape with healthy male role models who can provide guidance, support, and stability and change the picture inside them of the past.

Changing The Picture Inside

The picture that forms in one's mind due to loss or trauma can be bleak and limiting. However, by embracing relationships with nurturing male figures, these young individuals can reshape that image into one filled with strength, love, and resilience. A supportive dad-like figure can offer wisdom drawn from experience, teach valuable life lessons, and foster a sense of belonging many may crave.

I   t's essential to recognize that seeking out these relationships is courageous, not a sign of weakness. It demonstrates a commitment to personal growth and healing. By opening themselves up to new connections, they are taking proactive steps toward rewriting their narratives—turning pain into empowerment. So, let us champion this pursuit; finding a positive male influence could be the catalyst for profound change in their lives.

The Picture Of Father Inside

If the picture you have of a father is from a bad dad experience and does not change, it will inevitably affect how you perceive God's role in your life. Many men carry the weight of negative experiences with their fathers— whether through absence, sickness, or broken marriages— which shapes the filters through which they view relationships. This is especially poignant regarding understanding women and nurturing those vital connections.

One of the most damaging effects of having a bad dad is that it can distort your perception of God. When we associate our earthly fathers' shortcomings with divine characteristics, we risk projecting those flaws onto our understanding of love and support in our relationships.

To avoid this cycle, husbands must break free from these past experiences and embrace vulnerability. By doing so, they can foster an environment where emotional intimacy thrives—ultimately strengthening their marriages and allowing them to connect with their wives more deeply.

The concern I have for all concerned is that you may view God through the filters of your past hurtful or neglectful relationships. This perspective can profoundly hinder your desire to invite Him into your life, especially in moments when you seek divine intervention from God.

If you've experienced betrayal, abandonment, or indifference from those who were meant to care for you, it's understandable that you might project those feelings onto your perception of God. However, it's crucial to recognize that God is not a reflection of human failings; He embodies the ultimate love and compassion. By allowing past hurts to shape your understanding of His nature, you risk missing out on the profound relationship

He offers you. A relationship where He desires to be the best dad you could ever hope for. Embracing this truth requires a conscious effort to separate the pain of past experiences from the unconditional love and support that God provides.

Consider this: what if letting go of those filters could lead you to a deeper sense of peace and fulfillment? Imagine experiencing a father figure who is always present, endlessly forgiving, and genuinely invested in your well-being. By shifting your perspective and opening yourself up to God's true character, you can begin to heal from past wounds and cultivate a rich spiritual life filled with hope and purpose. Don't let previous disappointments dictate how you see Him; instead, allow His love to redefine what it means to be cared for unconditionally.

Good Dad Bad Dad

CHAPTER NINE

Male Role Models

When we think of role models for our children and the younger generation, it is greatly influenced by a good dad or a bad dad. A good dad is a better role model than a lousy dad, but both have lasting effects on the lives of the children. When we consider the role models for our children and the younger generation, the influence of a father cannot be overstated. A good dad is a cornerstone in a child's development, instilling values such as responsibility, empathy, resilience, accountability, and honesty.

Conversely, the impact of a bad dad is equally profound but often detrimental. Negative behaviors exhibited by fathers, such as neglect, aggression, or poor communication skills, can leave lasting scars on children. These experiences may lead to issues like low self-esteem or difficulties in forming healthy relationships later on. It's crucial to recognize that both types of father figures shape their children's perceptions of what it means to be an adult.

The Legacy Left By Good Dads

In light of this understanding, we must emphasize the importance of good fatherhood. Encouraging fathers to engage positively with their children not only benefits individual families but also strengthens communities at large.

By fostering and encouraging environments where good dads can thrive, and bad dads can seek help for their shortcomings, we will pave the way for healthier future generations who will carry these lessons into their parenting roles someday. Fathers' legacy is not just personal; it reverberates through society and shapes the future of us all.

Thus, this book does not promote one parenting style against another but champions the ideals of good parenting, with a particular emphasis on fatherhood. In today's world, where the role of fathers is evolving and often scrutinized, it's crucial to foster an environment that encourages positive change. My is that this book serves as a beacon of hope for dads who may find themselves in the "bad dad" category at any level—whether due to past mistakes or current struggles.

Seek The Hope of Change

Every father has the potential for growth and transformation. However, this change cannot occur until a dad takes a step back and honestly assesses his actions and intentions. Self-reflection is key; it allows fathers to identify areas needing improvement and seek resources or support systems to guide them toward better practices. By embracing this journey of self-discovery and accountability, fathers can not only improve their own lives but also create lasting positive impacts on their children's futures. This book aims to inspire those dads by providing practical advice, relatable stories, and encouragement every step of the way.

Mothers are Vital in Our Lives

I want to stress that I am focussing on the role of dads, but I am not underestimating the role of mothers. In discussing the pivotal role of fathers in a child's life, I want to emphasize that this focus does not diminish the invaluable contributions of mothers. The truth is that a mother without a supportive partner often faces significant challenges in providing balance and stability for her children; when a father is absent, whether due to absence or lack of engagement, it creates an imbalance that can affect the entire family dynamic.

A non-functioning husband presents significant hurdles. His presence might be felt, but mothers bear an uneven burden if he is not actively contributing to parenting and engaged in support. This reality underscores the urgent need for good dads—those who are committed, involved, and present in their children's lives. We must advocate for fathers who understand their vital role in nurturing healthy relationships within families.

By strengthening the focus on fatherhood and promoting active participation from dads, we can help create a more balanced environment where children can thrive. It's about time we recognized that engaged fathers are not just beneficial; they are essential for fostering emotional well-being in our youth.

The Positive Effects of Being a Good Role Model

Being a good role model is one of the most impactful contributions you can make to the lives of those around you, particularly in the context of positive parenting. Good role models' traits, such as integrity, empathy, resilience, and honesty, set a powerful example for children and young adults. When they observe nurturing behaviors in their parents or guardians, they are more likely to adopt these values themselves.

Children who grow up with strong role models are better equipped to navigate challenges and build healthy relationships. They learn the importance of kindness and responsibility through observation rather than instruction alone.

Actions Speak Louder Than Words

Actions speak louder than words, and this adage holds profound truth in our daily lives. Consider the age-old phrase, "Do what I say and not what I do." While it may seem like a harmless directive, the reality is far more complex. Children are keen observers; they absorb behaviors and attitudes from their parents, often mimicking actions rather than adhering strictly to verbal instructions.

As a child, I was deeply influenced by the advertisements that surrounded me, particularly one that starkly depicted parents indulging in drinking and smoking, only to cut to their children mimicking these behaviors in a cubby house. This advertisement served as a powerful reminder of the impact that adult actions can have on impressionable young minds.

Be Imitators of Me - Lead By Example

The Apostle Paul encouraged his disciples to imitate him. Wow, how many of us really want others to imitate us? This advertisement highlighted how children often emulate what they see, absorbing behaviors without understanding their consequences. The imagery of children pretending to drink and smoke shows impartation is more powerful than words of instruction. We must recognize that when a parent, mentor, or authority figure displays a contradiction of their words by their actions, it can lead to lasting impressions on children's perceptions of adulthood and feel it gives them permission.

We Receive By Impartation

God created us to receive by impartation mainly. This is more effective than education. When parents preach values like honesty or kindness but fail to embody these principles in their behavior, they send mixed messages that can confuse their children. For instance, if a parent emphasizes the importance of integrity while engaging in dishonest practices themselves, the child is likely to adopt those actions as their norm. This phenomenon extends beyond parenting; it permeates every aspect of our interactions—be it in leadership roles, friendships, or community engagements. The Bible instructs us to abstain from even the appearance of evil.

Actions Must Align With Words

Ultimately, if we want to inspire change or instill values in others, we must lead by example. Our actions must align with our words to create a consistent message that resonates with those around us. Can we genuinely influence and guide others toward positive behaviors and outcomes? In essence, the ripple effect of being a good role model cannot be underestimated; it creates lasting change that resonates far beyond our immediate circles.

Personal Story of Blue and Occa in Australia

Years ago, when we were selling up to move to the USA, we had a big garage sale to raise our airfares for the trip. As I had been the builder of my house and the church facility, I had lots of building tools for sale. Karen was looking after the sale of the furniture and household goods, and I had all my tools, nail guns, power tools, chop-saws, etc, in the garage. One day, a rough-looking tradesman turned up to buy some of the tools. They had typical Australian 'nicknames,' which is very common in Australia. Most names are shortened, or a typical nickname is adopted. The red-headed guy was called 'Blue,' and the other was called 'Occa.' Occa comes from an Aussie term, 'True blue Occa,' which means he is the real deal Aussie bloke. These two guys would be typical rednecks in America.

The Presence of God Changes The Atmosphere

Anyway, while these fellows were checking out the tools, they asked me if I was a builder, as I had all the tools. I said, "Not really." I am a minister of the church down the road, but I built the church and my home. Well, their reaction was spontaneous with wide eyes. Their response was not just that I was a minister; they recognized that something had changed in them when they walked into my garage and connected with me.

Blue said, "That explains it, mate; I was wondering why we stopped swearing when we came in here." Occa

103

responded, "Crikey, you're right, Blue; we usually fill the air with the F-bomb every other word."

I did not think too much about what they were saying until later, but it opened the door for me to share my faith and why we do what we do. In hindsight, I was not in any mood to witness about my faith as it was a tough time giving up everything we had to travel. But it showed me very clearly that when our faith walk is real, the atmosphere around our life and home changes. Jesus said His peace and presence would make a mark on our lives and rest within the home. He said even if someone gives a child of God a cup of water, they would not lose their reward. On another occasion, he said if a household receives you, leave your peace with that household. Impartation is real in our lives for good or for bad.

When our faith walk is genuine, the transformation in our lives and surroundings becomes unmistakable. Jesus promised that His peace and presence would serve as a defining mark on those who truly follow Him. This assurance is not just a comforting notion; it is a profound truth that resonates deeply within the fabric of our daily existence.

Consider this: even the simplest acts of kindness, like offering a cup of water to someone in need, carry significant weight in God's eyes. Jesus emphasized that such gestures do not go unnoticed; they are rewarded by Him. This principle extends beyond mere actions; it reflects the heart behind them, showing how our faith can inspire and uplift those around us.

Our homes can become sanctuaries filled with love and God's presence, with the potential to influence everyone who enters. The ripple effect of living out our faith can touch lives in ways we may never fully comprehend, but it starts with us wholeheartedly embracing that transformative journey. Let us strive to cultivate an environment where God's presence is felt vividly—after all, when our faith walk is real, everything around us begins to change for the better. Let it start in your life and home first.

Our House is God's Embassy

The word says we as believers are 'Christ Ambassadors.' If we are Ambassadors of Christ and His Kingdom, our lives, homes, and churches will become the embassy. Property of the 'Kingdom of God.'

"We are Christ's ambassadors, as though God were making his appeal through us. We implore you on Christ's behalf: Be reconciled to God ." 2 Corinthians 5:20

The United States maintains embassies around the globe, which serve as physical representations of American values and sovereignty. When you step through those gates, guarded by soldiers committed to protecting the nation's interests, you enter a space that embodies the principles of democracy and freedom. This is not just a building; it is an extension of America itself.

Similarly, a genuine relationship with God creates an atmosphere that permeates every aspect of life and home. Just as an embassy is a bastion of national identity and purpose, faith establishes a sanctuary for spiritual growth and connection. God's presence in your life is not merely abstract; it becomes tangible in the way you interact with others, face challenges, and cultivate peace within your surroundings.

This divine presence transforms ordinary moments into extraordinary experiences. It fosters resilience during trials and joy in everyday blessings. Much like how embassies serve to connect citizens with their homeland while abroad, a genuine faith connects us deeply to our God—providing guidance, comfort, and strength in all circumstances. Embrace this relationship wholeheartedly; let it reflect in your actions and interactions just as proudly as any flag flying over an embassy does around the world.

CHAPTER TEN

Story of a Bad Dad

Many years ago, I encountered a lady with a tragic childhood in my first pastoral position. This is an extreme story that I encountered as a young pastor. I was a young associate pastor in a church full of people with diverse backgrounds, cultures, and life experiences. In those days, I would make appointments to counsel people through my secretary, often taking an hour or more.

One morning, a middle-aged lady came for counsel concerning deep emotional problems. That were affecting her relationship with her husband. As I was leading her in prayer, I would often say in the name of Jesus, and she was responding well. I felt led to stop and just say to her, "You need to open to the father's love."

Well, you would think I shocked her with 240 volts as she screamed a blood-curdling scream. Then, in a wild panic, she exited my office, screaming as she ran down the hallway to the stairs. I was so shocked I took off after her, worried she would hurt herself or fall down the stairs, I caught up with her and almost tackled her just before the stairs. I comforted and led her back to my office, where my secretary helped calm her down.

Some time passed, and she seemed ready to talk, so I gently asked why she reacted so violently. Through tears, she began to tell me her tragic story concerning her father's abuse of her and her older brother. I will not go into all the graphic details here, but as she told me the story, I could hardly hold back my tears.

In those days, I was a little naive as to how many people had terrible experiences with their fathers. After some time, she got to the part of the story that shocked me. She said the abuse was so bad that she and her brother had planned to shoot their dad to escape his abuse by using their dad's rifle.

She said her dad would often play 'Russian Roulette' with her after swinging her around the room by her pony tail. Her 'bad dad' would approach her very drunk and with his rifle pointing at her, pulling the trigger several times and then pointing it slightly away blowing a hole through the old farmhouse wall, just missing her.

Eventually, it was just too much for these young kids, so one morning, while he was shaving, they surprised their dad in the bathroom and took his life with a shot. Without going into the graphic details, this was a tragic, traumatic experience for any child beyond the daily abuse of years from this 'Bad dad,' who grossly mistreated his responsibility to protect his kids.

It was a wake-up call to realize that not everyone has an image of a loving father they can trust to care for them. I then understood why she felt safe talking about Jesus as a big brother, but when I suggested a relationship with Father God, she exploded in fear. It was like a trigger that unleashed a wild panic attack.

Over time, this precious lady was healed and freed from her tragic past. I never met her brother, but if you were wondering if they were charged with their father's murder, they were not. Not only were they very young at the time of this incident, but when the truth came out about the constant abuse, the judge deemed them to be victims of extreme physical and emotional abuse and not charged. I need to say that although the court set them free lawfully, this precious wife and mother was still imprisoned by the strongholds of the memories until her Good (Heavenly) Dad set her free.

This was the first of many encounters I would have with messed up adults whose tragic stories were rooted in parental abuse in their younger days. Each story was a testament to the profound impact that early experiences can have on an individual's life. However, amidst the heartache and despair, there is a beacon of hope. The good news of the Gospel opens a door wide to the possibility of real help, healing, and freedom from any person's past by a loving Heavenly Father. God also co-works with ministers that understand what He has provided to set people free, as he did with me through this experience.

Clearly, there is no quick fix for such tragic experiences, but I can honestly say with God's help and persistent hope from the promises in God's word, lives can change dramatically.

Establishing Your Freedom

These real tragedies are not easy to talk about. That's why I do not use anyone's name, but the dramatic freedom that was made available to them is available to others. We defeat the enemy's works by the blood of the lamb and the word of our testimony, the word declares.

Revelation 12:11-16 NIV. *"They triumphed over him by the blood of the Lamb and by the word of their testimony."*

That is why we share testimonies as they expose the dark works of the enemy. I've witnessed how understanding the promises in God's word combined with faith and perseverance restores broken lives, and I want to shout it from the rooftops.

There are many bible teachers today who discredit the 'Full Gospel' that includes the powerful message of the cross and how we co-work with the Holy Spirit to set people free. Jesus came to free the captives. The Bible says those who are set free by the Spirit of God are free indeed, which means free in reality.

"The Spirit of the LORD is upon Me Because He has anointed Me To preach the gospel to the poor; He has sent Me to heal the brokenhearted, To proclaim liberty to the captives And recovery of sight to the blind, To set at liberty those who are oppressed." Luke 4:18

"Stand fast therefore in the liberty by which Christ has made us free, and do not be entangled again with a yoke of bondage." Galatians 5:1

This declares the freedom of Christ's death and resurrection accomplished through the cross. The profound Message of the Cross is what we will examine as we work through God's plan of salvation and freedom from the molestation of our souls' enemies.

I share these stories to illuminate the issues confronting so many people. It's incredible how many issues are caused by or rooted in the influence of a 'Bad Dad' and how many children are protected by experiencing their upbringing with a 'Good Dad.'

It's essential to recognize that while memories may remain, they have lost their power over you after God heals you. Memories do not keep your past in the secrecy of darkness but rather expose it to the light. Instead of being shackled by our pasts, we can reclaim our lives and move towards brighter futures filled with hope and possibility.

Beyond The Darkness is Hope

However, amid these experiences' darkness, there is hope and healing. The good news is that with prayer and God's intervention, many have found a path to recovery and restoration.

Stories of those who have faced parental abuse often reveal a journey marked by struggle but ultimately lead to transformation when they invite God into the journey. Individuals who once felt trapped in cycles of pain have discovered strength through their faith. Prayer becomes a lifeline, offering solace and guidance during the most challenging times. It connects them to God's power through the working of the Holy Spirit to provide comfort, peace, and increasing freedom.

Many people recount moments where they felt an undeniable presence guiding them towards healing as a result of counseling, understanding the guidance and strength revealed in scripture. These divine interventions remind us that no one is alone in their suffering; there is always hope for renewal, knowing that God is near to the broken soul.

These stories also highlight the workings of God in the human spirit when bolstered by faith. Healing is possible, even from the deepest wounds inflicted by those we trust the most. By embracing prayer and seeking God's help, individuals can reclaim their God-given destiny and find peace beyond their pasts.

The road may be long, but with prayer as a guide and God's love as a foundation, recovery from parental abuse can lead to profound personal transformation and newfound joy in life.

CHAPTER ELEVEN

Childhood Trauma

Childhood trauma and forms of abuse inflicted by parents or adult figures have far-reaching consequences that can shape a child's future in profound ways. The impact of such experiences is not merely confined to the early years; it reverberates throughout their lives, affecting their emotional health, relationships, and overall well-being.

Children who endure trauma often struggle with trust issues, finding it difficult to form healthy attachments later in life. The scars of abuse can manifest as anxiety, depression, and low self-esteem, hindering their ability to navigate social situations or maintain intimate relationships. If you identify with this in any way, my message to you is that there is a way to be healed and restored through faith and patience, embracing the truths of scripture that I am addressing throughout this book.

Hurt People Hurt People

This cycle of pain from abuse can perpetuate itself if left unaddressed, as individuals may unconsciously replicate harmful patterns they experienced during childhood. It has become apparent to me that many people who abuse others were themselves products of abuse in their lives. This troubling reality highlights the urgent need for awareness and intervention.

When trauma goes unacknowledged, it festers and transforms into a cycle that ensnares not just the individual but also those around them. The behaviors learned in childhood—whether through direct experience or observation—often manifest in adulthood, creating a vicious cycle of hurt that can span generations. Abusers may not even recognize their actions as harmful; instead, they see them as normal responses to the pain they endured.

Break The Cycle Of Pain

Breaking this cycle is paramount. It requires a commitment to healing and self-awareness that many find daunting, but it is so necessary. Individuals can begin dismantling these ingrained patterns by addressing past traumas through prayer, support groups, counseling ministry, and educational resources. Understanding that abuse begets abuse is the first step toward breaking free from this destructive legacy. We must encourage open conversations about personal histories in environments where healing is prioritized over silence.

Many Suffer in Silence

Many individuals who have endured any form of abuse find themselves trapped in silence, grappling with feelings of shame and fear. The weight of their experiences often feels insurmountable, leading them to believe that sharing their story is not an option. This silence is compounded when the abuser is someone deemed trustworthy—often a family member or close family associate—creating a profound sense of betrayal that makes it even harder to speak out.

The stigma surrounding abuse can be paralyzing. Victims may worry that they won't be believed, or they might fear the repercussions of coming forward, especially when the abuser holds a position of power within the family structure. This reluctance to open up can perpetuate cycles of trauma and isolation, leaving individuals feeling alone in their suffering.

It's crucial to foster environments where survivors feel safe and supported in sharing their stories in a safe environment. We need to empower those who have been harmed to reclaim their dignity without fear or shame and thus create pathways for healing and restoration.

My Story Of Abuse When I Was Young

When I was 14 years of age, I experienced a traumatic event that would shape my understanding of trust and Christianity for many years. I was abused by the minister who had taken my grandfather's funeral. We were not church-going people then, so we did not know this man before the funeral.

The minister did a great job at the funeral and told my mum that he had a young man with whom he had played racket ball (Squash in Australia). He told my mum that this young man had gone to university and wondered if I would like to play a game with him.

To make things worse, my mum kept saying what a wonderful minister he was and what a great eulogy he had spoken about my grandpa. I reluctantly agreed to keep Mum happy.

I will not go into the details, but by the end of the game, he insisted we shower in this dingy place. I said I did not need to, as we had a pool at home, and I would go for a swim when I got home. He persisted, and out of embarrassment, I agreed, and this led to an embarrassing, abusive situation.

As a young boy, I was pretty innocent. I knew this was messed up, but it confused me because he was supposed to be a man of God. When we got home, Mum raved about how nice he was, so I just shut up and hoped I would not see him again.

After a couple of weeks, I arrived home from school, and the minister was in our home. He had bought birthday gifts for me, including a squash racket and a box of Swiss chocolates. I could not handle his presence or his gifts, and stormed out quickly and went to the garage extremely upset and angry. I started bashing something against the workbench when my older brother turned up behind me and asked what the matter was. He saw me leave and knew I was upset. I could not tell him for a while, but he persisted and just said it is that man, isn't it.... I broke down and told him what happened. My big brother said to me, "You wait here. I am going to Dad, and he will deal with this." As my brother headed back inside, I immediately felt relief, knowing my dad would do something.

My grandma lived two houses down from us, and I saw my dad fly out to address this man on my behalf. I never really asked Dad what he did that day, but later that night, my dad and mum brought this up around the family table, and we talked it out till I was lifted out of my hurt and confusion.

That was a big part of my healing that day because, as a family, we brought this whole matter into the light with healthy discussion until the embarrassment, shame, and confusion were lifted. I was so grateful to have a good dad to help me through all this. In hindsight, this incident possibly kept me critical of Christianity and church because when the subject of God or church came up, I equated it with this minister and his abuse.

We were not Christian in those early days, so we did not know about prayer. Many years later, I received more profound healing through prayer from the deeper abuse on my soul. I did not realize how much this incident affected me until I received this deeper healing.

Now I have a good heavenly dad with a big brother, Jesus, who went to the Father on my behalf, just like my earthly brother went to my earthly dad to defend and heal me.

Many abused People Can Not Share Their Experience Of Abuse.

It is a fact that many individuals suffering from abuse remain silent, often trapped in a cycle of fear and confusion. I was in that place until my brother intervened. The reasons for this silence are complex and deeply rooted in trust and power dynamics. Often, the abuser is someone deemed to be a trusted family member or an acquaintance, an individual who is woven into the very fabric of daily life.

This complicates the victim's ability to speak out; they may fear disbelief, shame, or even retaliation, and the emotional turmoil can be overwhelming. Victims grapple with conflicting feelings about their abuser, who may also play a significant role in their lives as a family member, caretaker, or mentor.

This duality creates an internal struggle that can lead to isolation and despair. It's crucial to recognize that silence is not consent; it is often a cry for help muffled by fear. I understand this struggle deeply; it was a battle I faced myself for years. Even though in my experience of abuse, I had an open dialogue with my dad and family, I held that part of my life in a secret place until I was set completely free through prayer.

As a minister, I shared pretty much every negative experience in my life in a very transparent way over many years, to help others with my testimony of healing, growth, and freedom, but for some reason unknown at the time, I never shared about the minister abusing me as a young boy.

Public Sharing Of My Abuse

Until one night, I was teaching on the subject of 'Understanding Forgiveness' in a crowd of about six hundred people. To my surprise, after all these years and thousands of meetings, I began to share my story of abuse publicly. As an inspirational preacher, I often drew from my own life experiences in my sermons, but this particular story remained shrouded in secrecy for far too long. In hindsight, I realized that I believed it was too personal to divulge. However, the truth is starkly different: I harbored deep-seated hurt and allowed it to create a stronghold within me—locking away my pain and keeping me imprisoned by my past. I felt I would be judged by my critics, but that was just an excuse to keep this stronghold safe.

I remember that night so clearly, as I came to the close of my sermon, grappling with the weight of finally sharing a profoundly personal experience after so many years in ministry. It was a moment filled with vulnerability and courage, one that resonated with many in the congregation who had also faced their struggles with abuse. I appealed to the congregation to come to the altar for healing through the forgiveness of the perpetrators of the offense.

I remember saying that I had never shared this story before, so it must be God wanting me to share it with people in the meeting. As I called people forward, to my amazement, over two-thirds of the crowd moved to the altar. As I led them through prayer to forgive their abusers, weeping and wailing and rivers of tears filled the auditorium as we asked our Heavenly Father to break the bondage of un-forgiveness.

Breaking The Bondage Of Unforgiveness

There were hundreds of people set free that night from all age groups, from the young to the very old, both men and women.

I was overwhelmed by how many people were set free that night because I shared my personal experience, which opened them up to God's deep healing and restoration as a result of this unplanned testimony. By finally speaking out about my experience, I've discovered healing for myself and the power of vulnerability in connecting with others who have endured similar struggles. It's essential for those suffering in silence to recognize that there is a clear path to healing and restoration from a good, good 'Heavenly Father.'

If you are a victim of abuse in your past, facing and uncovering your personal story with someone who has an understanding of how the Holy Spirit can break the bondage of un-forgiveness can be liberating and transformative for you also. You are not alone; countless others resonate with your pain and are waiting for someone brave enough to break the silence.

That night was a turning point, not just for those who were set free but for me as well. As I began to share my story of abuse publicly, I felt an overwhelming sense of liberation wash over me. Although I had often drawn upon my experiences as an inspirational preacher, this particular story had remained hidden—too personal and too painful to reveal. In hindsight, it became clear that the very act of keeping this part of my life locked away was what kept me imprisoned by my past.

I realized that by opening up about my hurt and the stronghold it created within me, I could help others experience God's deep healing and restoration. The moment I shared my truth, something remarkable happened: not only did many find their freedom in hearing my story, but I, too, found healing in an area of my life that had been buried for over 35 years.

This experience taught me that vulnerability can be a powerful catalyst, not just in our own lives but in the lives of those around us. When we dare to share our struggles in the right environment, we invite others into a space where they can confront their pain and discover hope through God's grace.

By acknowledging this reality, we can begin to dismantle the barriers that prevent individuals from seeking help and healing from their trauma. It's time we listen, support, and advocate for those who have been hurt but remain unheard in their silence. If you are fighting back the tears as you are reading this because you have faced abuse or you have hurt someone else from your hurt, there is grace and forgiveness to be found that will heal and restore you to a place of freedom and peace.

If we collectively acknowledge this painful truth and work towards healing ourselves, we can disrupt this cycle of pain and create a brighter future for ourselves and generations to come. It's time to confront our pasts so we can stop repeating them—because everyone deserves a chance at a healthier life free from the shadows of abuse.

Moreover, the effects are not limited to emotional struggles; they can also impact physical health. Studies have shown that those who experience childhood trauma are at a higher risk for chronic illnesses in adulthood. This stark reality underscores the importance of recognizing and addressing the signs of abuse early on.

By fostering awareness and creating safe environments for healing, we can help break this cycle and empower survivors to reclaim their lives and dignity. Understanding the devastating effects of childhood trauma is the first step towards healing – both for individuals and for our communities as a whole.

Good Dad Bad Dad

CHAPTER TWELVE

Nothing Impossible For My Dad

As a son, I have embraced the profound quality of hope and trust my dad instilled since childhood. Life is often a journey filled with challenges and uncertainties, yet my upbringing taught me that no matter what obstacles we face, there is always a way through. I shared earlier that my dad seemed to embrace every obstacle with an attitude that there was a way to get through or get it done. This unwavering belief isn't just a personal experience for the few as it reflects the essence of the life that Father God offers to each of us today.

God's word promises to be a Father to the fatherless. Most of the story of the Bible is one of 'Sonship' and God's desire to adopt us as sons. Regardless of our past experiences—be they filled with joy or marked by struggle—this divine promise remains steadfast. It invites us to rise above our circumstances and embrace a future illuminated by hope. Just as my parents taught me to trust in the possibilities ahead, we are all called to recognize that the same assurance is available through faith. In Mark 9:23 it says, "If you can believe, all things *are* possible to him who believes." In Luke 1:37 it states, " For with God nothing will be impossible." So, nothing is impossible for God, and as a result, nothing will be impossible for us if we believe that God can perform what he has promised. That was the faith of Abraham that eventually got his son of promise, Isaac.

Nothing Has The Power to Separate God's Love from Us

Romans 8:35-39 says that nothing will separate us from the love of God and gives a comprehensive list of things that try to separate Him from us, with a promise that it can not!

"Who shall separate us from the love of Christ? Shall tribulation, or distress, or persecution, or famine, or nakedness, or peril, or sword? .... Yet in all these things, we are more than conquerors through Him who loved us. For I am persuaded that neither death nor life, nor angels nor principalities nor powers, nor things present nor things to come, nor height nor depth, nor any other created thing, shall be able to separate us from the love of God which is in Christ Jesus our Lord.

In other words, nothing in all creation can separate God and His love and provision from you. This profound truth is woven throughout scripture, reminding us of the unwavering nature of God's commitment to us. However, it is crucial to understand that while nothing external can sever this bond between Father God and us, we can create distance from God through our choices. The old saying goes, ' *If you feel distant from God, guess who moved?'*

Scriptural teachings reveal various ways we can actively engage with God's love and provision—through faith, obedience, and prayer. These practices not only deepen our relationship with Him but also align us with His abundant blessings. It's vital to recognize that when we stray from these paths or allow doubt and fear to creep in, we inadvertently separate ourselves from the very source of love and support meant for us.

Father God will Always Pick You Up When You Fall

The beauty lies in the fact that no matter how far we feel we've wandered, God's arms are always open wide, ready to welcome us back into His embrace.

In Psalm 37:24 it states, *"Though we fall, He shall not be utterly cast down; For the LORD upholds him with His hand."*

Embrace this truth that while you may influence or weaken your connection with God from your side of the relationship, through your actions or mindset, His love remains steadfast and unchanging—a constant beacon guiding you homeward to be comforted and cared for. Your Heavenly Father will not hold your transgression against you.

Therefore, it is crucial to recognize and understand that while nothing can sever God's love from us, we have the power to distance ourselves from it through our thoughts and actions.

The way you think about yourself, your circumstances, and your relationship with God plays a pivotal role in how you experience His love. Negative self-talk or doubt can create barriers that obscure the warmth of His presence. When we allow fear or insecurity to dominate our mindset, we inadvertently push away the very love that is always available to us.

Past Hurts And Abuse Creates a Barrier of Trust

Past hurts and abuses from father figures create deep-seated barriers of trust, particularly towards authority figures, that act like a filter that blurs 'God's Love' from our perspective. This skepticism limits our ability to embrace His love fully. When we've been let down or harmed by those in positions of power or trust, it's only natural to project that pain onto our perception of divine authority. However, it is crucial to recognize that God is not like the flawed humans who may have caused us harm. He embodies unconditional love and acceptance, free from the biases and failures we've experienced in the past.

130

By acknowledging these barriers, we can begin to allow the Holy Spirit to dismantle them—allowing ourselves to open up to the transformative power of God's love.

Healing requires courage. It involves confronting painful memories and redefining our understanding of authority. Embracing God's love means trusting He sees beyond our scars and desires a relationship that transcends past experiences. The journey may be challenging, but breaking down these walls can lead to profound spiritual growth and a renewed sense of belonging in His embrace. Every child wants to be loved and needs a good dad.

You Must Open The Door

The fact is, God is waiting patiently at your door, ready to enter your life and transform your situation. Imagine a loving figure standing just outside, hopeful and eager to bring peace, guidance, and support into your world. But here's the catch: you have to make the first move. It's not enough to simply acknowledge His presence; you must actively approach the door and open it.

"Here I am! I stand at the door and knock. If anyone hears my voice and opens the door, I will come in and eat with that person, and they with me. " Revelations 3:20

This act of opening the door symbolizes your willingness to invite 'divine intervention' into your

131

circumstances. Whether you're facing challenges in relationships, career struggles, or personal doubts, taking that step toward God can lead to profound changes. He won't force Himself in; instead, He waits for you to seek Him out.

In moments of despair or uncertainty, remember that you are not alone—God is right there with you, standing at the door of your heart. By choosing to engage with Him through prayer or reflection, you allow His light to shine on even the darkest corners of your life. So take that brave step today; move towards the door and open it wide. The transformation you've been longing for is just a decision away.

Prayer: '*Father God, please forgive me for separating in any way from your love; I draw near to you in my weakness; I open the door to your help and loving kindness and ask you to set me free from the barriers of my past so I can walk in the light of your love and grace.*'

If you prayed that prayer to Father God from your heart, He is already working on the answer. Embracing a mindset rooted in faith that God is faithful to his word allows us to fully engage with God's unwavering support and provision.

Remember, it's not about changing who you are at this point, but instead aligning your thoughts with the truth of God's promises—because when you do so, you're opening the door wide for His love to flow freely into your life and bring the very real possibility of change that we all long for. Let us hold fast to this truth: no matter where we've been or what we've faced, there is always a way forward grounded in faith and trust.

Remember: 'It's Only Theory Until You Do it'…. Dougs book that is also on Amazon

CHAPTER THIRTEEN

Love Voids

Bad dads can create profound love voids in their children's lives, leading to emotional scars that may last a lifetime if not recognized. These voids manifest as feelings of abandonment, low self-esteem, and difficulty forming healthy relationships. Children who grow up with absent or neglectful fathers often struggle with trust issues and may carry a deep-seated longing for the affection they miss out on.

Importance of a Father's Love

A father's love is vital in any child's life. It is part of God's grand design, creating a need in every person, young or old. I believe that is why God introduces himself to Christians as 'Our Father.' Despite popular liberal thoughts, He did not introduce Himself as 'Mother God.' Understanding the importance of a father in all our lives opens the door wide for Father God to fill the voids and bring wholeness.

It is essential to recognize that healing is possible. Many find solace in faith and spirituality, believing God can fill these voids with unconditional love and acceptance. Through prayer, individuals can begin to mend the wounds left by their father's absence. God's love offers a transformative power that helps restore hope.

In acknowledging these painful experiences while embracing the possibility of healing through divine intervention, we empower ourselves to seek fulfillment beyond our past. Those affected by such voids must understand they are not alone; there is a path towards wholeness that leads directly into the embrace of a loving Father who understands their pain.

A father's love is not just a comforting presence; it is a fundamental pillar in every child's emotional and spiritual development. This love embodies strength, guidance, and stability, which are crucial for nurturing well-rounded individuals. The significance of a father's role can be traced back to the creation design itself. As I said, God intentionally chose to reveal Himself as 'Our Father' in Christian theology, emphasizing the importance of paternal love in our lives.

In this context, it's essential to recognize that God's choice was deliberate and meaningful. While modern liberal perspectives may advocate for alternative interpretations of divine identity, the traditional understanding underscores that a father's love fulfills a profound need within each person, young or old. This paternal connection fosters trust, security, and resilience. It shapes how we perceive authority and cultivates relationships throughout our lives.

Rejecting this notion diminishes fathers' unique contributions to their children's growth. A father's influence encompasses mentorship and moral guidance that help shape character and instill values. Embracing God as 'Our Father' reinforces divine love—an irreplaceable aspect of God's grand design for your healing.

How are Love Voids Healed - First Step

The first step is to acknowledge that you have these love voids of a father's love. In the journey of everyone's life, many individuals encounter what can be described as "love voids"—those profound feelings of emptiness or lack of connection. These voids often stem from past traumas, moral abuse, spoken abuse, broken relationships, or unmet emotional needs. The healing power of God offers a transformative path to fill these gaps with God's genuine love and fulfillment.

A deep Relationship with God

God heals love voids by first inviting us into a deeper relationship with Him to save us eternally. Then He saves us from our past to render it powerless. Through prayer, this divine connection with Father God provides comfort and nurtures our spirit, addressing our souls that have been damaged by granting forgiveness—both for ourselves and others. Then as we let go of past hurts and resentments, our spirit opens to receive new love and real connection with our loving father.

This surrender is not always easy but is essential for healing; it allows God's grace to flow freely into our lives. Then, we are embraced by those who love and accept us in church.

That is the basis of the church to gather his kids with a common bond of a Father's love. That's what should make us a strong church family. When the church does not provide this environment, it is usually directly or indirectly a result of wrong teaching.

Ultimately, when we invite God into the process of healing our love voids, we begin to experience restoration that transcends human understanding—a profound sense of belonging that fills every empty space within us. Trusting in this divine journey allows us to emerge stronger and more capable of loving others deeply.

Submission is a Choice, and Vital

Healing Love Voids by God is a transformative journey that begins with acknowledging the emptiness within. The first step is to face the reality of your void;

138

recognizing it is crucial for genuine healing. Without this acknowledgment, you may continue to carry the weight of unfulfilled emotional needs and past wounds.

Next, submission to His gospel is essential. Embracing the teachings of Christ allows you to open your heart to divine love and grace. This submission isn't about surrendering your identity but allowing God's love to fill the spaces where hurt once resided. It's an act of faith that invites healing into your life. This means surrendering your pain and past experiences to Him and trusting in His plan for your life.

Seek understanding to change the picture your past painted. Delve into scripture, pray, and surround yourself with a supportive community that reflects God's love. Through this understanding, you can reinterpret your experiences and see how they have shaped you — not as a victim but as a vessel for growth and resilience to be free.

By taking these steps, you will heal and cultivate a deeper relationship with God, transforming your voids into sources of strength and hope. Embracing His teachings will give you the strength and guidance needed. Remember, God's love fills every gap; it can heals insurmountable wounds.

Remember, God came to heal the Brokenhearted

Here are some Bible verses that mention healing the brokenhearted: You need to meditate on these scriptures till you are convinced in your Spirit that God is not only there for you, He is committed to be your healer.

- **Psalm 147:3**: "He heals the brokenhearted and binds up their wounds."

- **Psalm 34:18**: "The LORD is close to the brokenhearted and saves those who are crushed in spirit."

- **Psalm 51:19**: "A broken and crushed heart, O' God, you will not despise."

- **Psalm 55:22**: "Cast your burden on the Lord, and he will sustain you; he will never permit the righteous to be moved."

It is clear from scripture that God not only recognizes that there are broken and bruised people, but he desires to come close and heal them. Be convinced in your heart and pursue his love.

CHAPTER FOURTEEN

The Message Of The Cross

T he Message of the Cross of Christ is a profound testament of hope, redemption, and unconditional love. This message encapsulates the promise that no matter how far we stray or how deep our struggles run, there is always a path back to grace with God's Loving intervention. The cross symbolizes both sacrifice and victory—victory over sin, despair, and death itself.

Divine Forgiveness

One of the most compelling promises in this message is the assurance of forgiveness. Christ offers us a chance to start anew through His suffering and ultimate sacrifice on the cross for you. This promise invites us into a relationship where guilt and shame can be transformed into peace and purpose. Furthermore, the cross reminds us that we are never alone in our trials; Christ bears our burdens now because, by faith in what he accomplished on the cross, his help is ever available. Please note his works are requested by faith and are not automatic. Everything that was accomplished on the cross for you must be appropriated by faith and choice.

The Message of the Cross also encourages us to live with hope for eternal life—a promise that transcends our earthly existence. It calls us to embrace faith over fear and love over hatred. By accepting this message, we unlock personal transformation and an opportunity to impact those around us positively.

The older I get, the promise of eternal life beyond this earthly life is such an encouragement to stay true to my faith. When we embrace the promises woven into the fabric of the cross, we find strength in adversity and joy in service. The Message of the Cross is not merely historical; it is alive today, inviting each of us to experience its transformative power in our lives.

The verse in the Bible that mentions the message of the cross is 1 Corinthians 1:18, which states,

"For the message of the cross is folly to those who are perishing, but to us who are being saved it is the power of God."

The Bible says the message of the cross is a stumbling block to many, but it is the power of God for those who are being saved. The passage also says that God chose the foolish and weak of the world to shame the wise and strong. Lots to think about here.

Natural Mans Religion

For many, the message of the cross is indeed a stumbling block—difficult to grasp and often rejected by those who rely solely on human wisdom and strength. I call this the natural man's religion. Yet for those who are being saved, it is nothing short of the power of God. This contrast of interpretation invites us to reflect deeply on our understanding of the strength and wisdom that God makes available. The Bible says that God's wisdom makes the wisdom of the world look foolish.

Wisdom of the World vs God's Wisdom

Consider how God deliberately chose what is foolish and weak in the world to confound the wise and strong. This choice challenges our notions about success and intelligence. It encourages us to embrace humility, recognizing that true power lies not in our achievements or intellect but in our willingness to submit to God's divine purpose and plan for our lives.

The cross stands as a symbol not just of sacrifice but also of an invitation. An invitation to find strength in vulnerability and wisdom in what may seem foolish according to worldly standards.

143

I have been profoundly disappointed in many of the modern church teachings that have distorted the spiritual truth that has the power to set people free from their past.

If The Cross Be Emptied Of It's Power

Many of the professing church leaders of today have watered down or lost the message of the cross. The Bible warns that the message of the cross can be emptied of its power.

"For Christ did not send me to baptize, but to preach the gospel—not with wisdom and eloquence, lest the cross of Christ be emptied of its power." 1 Corinthian 1:17

From this scripture, it is essential to note that this message has power—*the power to forgive, save, set captives free, and* restore what has been lost. This verse highlights that while eloquence and wisdom may captivate an audience, the unadulterated truth of the gospel holds transformative power.

This message carries immense significance; it embodies the power to forgive sins, offering redemption to those burdened by guilt. It can save souls from despair and eternal separation from God. The gospel breaks chains of abuse, setting captives free from addiction, fear, and hopelessness. Moreover, it restores broken lives and relationships, healing where pain once existed.

The Gospel's Strength Lies In Its Simplicity

We must not lose sight of this powerful truth in a world saturated with distractions and competing theologies. The gospel's strength lies in its simplicity — it's not about how well we articulate our faith but about sharing the life-changing message that Christ's sacrifice brings hope and renewal. Embrace this calling to preach boldly. Let us not dilute its impact with human wisdom but instead allow its divine power to resonate in every heart willing to listen.

Time To Put On Our Big Boy Pants

"Brothers and sisters, stop thinking like children. In regard to evil be infants, but in your thinking be adults." 1 Corinthians 14:20

In this verse, Paul is teaching the Corinthians not to be immature in their thinking. He wants them to keep their innocence, especially when it comes to evil ideas and practices. However, he also wants them to learn to think and act with spiritual maturity. In other words, grow up guys!

Paul's message in this verse is similar to what he wrote in 1 Corinthians 3:1, where he described the Corinthians as *"infants in Christ."* He may also have been echoing Jesus' instructions in Matthew 10:16: *"I am sending you out like sheep among wolves. Therefore be as shrewd as snakes and as innocent as doves"*. These scriptures convey the thought that Jesus spoke to His disciples when he said, "Be like these children for such is the Kingdom of God." a child has innocence and trust without question.

In context, Paul is addressing childlike or immature use of spiritual gifts in the church, with a call to be mature in handling spiritual matters. In my experience, much of the professing church does not even believe the gifts of the Holy Spirit discussed here are relevant for today.

The word makes a statement in Romans 1:22— *"Although they claimed to be wise, they became fools."* In Psalm 14:1 it says, *"The fool says in his heart, there is no God."* I do not believe it is saying that people who are immature in spiritual matters are fools, but when we miss what God is saying and what He has provided for our obvious benefit, it is foolishness. The Bible refers to this person as one without the spirit. In other words, a person who is not discerning the word of God with the Holy Spirit of God.

"The person without the Spirit does not accept the things that come from the Spirit of God but considers them foolishness, and cannot understand them because they are discerned only through the Spirit. When we disregard what is precious about God or from God, it is foolishness. Acting like we know when we do not know. Trusting God in His word like an innocent child believing what his dad said to be true." 1 Corinthians 2:14

The person without spiritual discernment considers spiritual things foolish because they cannot understand them without spiritual discernment gained from the Holy Spirit within a man. They cannot understand what God is saying, why He is saying it, or its benefit.

Consider this: Having a map to find your way without a Compass to show true direction is like having a Bible without the Holy Spirit. The divine presence of the Holy Spirit within us acts as a guide, revealing deeper meanings and insights that transcend mere intellectual understanding. It opens our eyes to the richness of God's wisdom and helps us appreciate His plans for us. Therefore, it's crucial to cultivate this relationship with the Holy Spirit. By doing so, we enhance our ability to discern spiritual matters and recognize their significance in our lives.

When people ask if the gifts of the spirit are for today, I ask this simple question: what would be the point of a gift of healing if it was not for the church today if we will not need healing in heaven? The reality of Christ's ministry to the world was a spiritual man speaking and doing spiritual works.

Healing from God transcends mere physical restoration; it embodies hope, compassion, and divine intervention in our lives. The question arises: what would be the point of such a powerful gift if not for its application in our current world?

In heaven, we will experience complete wholeness and perfection—no pain, no suffering. However, here on Earth, we face trials and tribulations that can leave us feeling broken and lost. The gift of healing is a testament to God's love and mercy for His people during these challenging times. It equips the church to be a beacon of light in a world often filled with darkness.

Healing is not just about physical ailments; it's also about spiritual renewal and emotional restoration. The church acts as a vessel through which God's healing power flows into our communities, offering comfort to those who are hurting. Therefore, it is essential that we recognize the significance of all the spiritual gifts and all that God has made available to the church today. Otherwise, the message of the cross is emptied of its power.

The Purity And Simplicity Of Christ

The Kingdom of God was introduced through Jesus Christ with signs and wonders to demonstrate Father God's love for his broken and lost creation. Jesus was the manifestation of His Spiritual Father in a physical body to demonstrate spiritual love and care in the physical world.

The Kingdom of God was profoundly introduced to humanity through the life and ministry of Jesus Christ, marked by an extraordinary display of signs and wonders that serve as a testament to Father God's immense love for His broken and lost creation. These miraculous acts were not mere spectacles for a moment in time as some would say; they were divine affirmations of hope, healing, and redemption aimed at a world steeped in despair.

Consider the countless lives transformed by Jesus' miracles—blind eyes opened, the lame walking, and even the dead being raised. Each act was a powerful declaration that God sees our pain and intervenes with compassion. Through these signs, Jesus revealed the nature of His Father and His Kingdom: one where love triumphs over suffering, grace over judgment, and restoration over destruction.

Signs and wonders that vividly illustrated the profound love of Father God for His broken and lost creation. This divine intervention was not merely a display of power; it was a heartfelt invitation to humanity to experience reconciliation and restoration, to be ready for His everlasting Kingdom at the end of this age.

Jesus embodied the very essence of His Spiritual Father, taking on human form to demonstrate love, compassion, and care in a tangible physical way. Through miracles, healing the sick, feeding the hungry, and even raising the dead. He revealed a God who is deeply invested in our physical lives. These acts were not just random occurrences; they were intentional demonstrations meant to draw us into an understanding of God's true nature.

In a world often filled with pain and suffering, Jesus' ministry serves as a beacon of hope. It reminds us that we are not alone in our struggles; rather, we are cherished by a Creator who desires to mend our brokenness. The Kingdom He proclaimed is one where spiritual love transcends earthly limitations, offering us both comfort and transformation. Embracing this truth invites us into a deeper relationship with God—a relationship characterized by trust in His unwavering love amidst life's challenges.

Moreover, these wonders made available through the finished work of the cross were meant to invite us into a relationship with God—a loving Father who desires to mend our brokenness. The presence of such miraculous power is not just historical, as some want us to believe, but continues today as many believers experience personal transformations in their lives.

As we explore this profound introduction to God's Kingdom through Christ, we are reminded that His love is both transformative and accessible.

All this to say, your healing and restoration are available to you today as you grasp and appropriate the amazing provision of what God accomplished through the cross because of His great love for you! The message of the cross is a love letter from you, good dad in Heaven, saying come home, kids, and find safety, healing, peace, and comfort, now and forever!

CHAPTER FIFTEEN

The Power Of God's Forgiveness

Understanding the transformative power of God's supernatural forgiveness is essential for anyone seeking liberation from the bondage of darkness. This divine act is not merely a human endeavor; it is God Himself releasing forgiveness through you, creating a shift in your soul. It saves your soul little by little, returning it to you. When we embrace His supernatural forgiveness, we are cleansed of our past toxic memories of bad events and empowered to rebuild on a clean foundation.

Imagine the weight lifted off your shoulders as you allow God's love to flow through you, breaking chains of resentment and bitterness. They have been locked up for years. This release transforms hearts and minds, enabling individuals to enter a new life filled with hope and purpose.

By understanding that forgiveness originates from God, we can recognize its power in dismantling strongholds that have kept us trapped in darkness for so long.

Accepting God's supernatural forgiveness transforms us into vessels of His grace, reflecting His light into the lives of those around us. This transformative process heals our wounds and creates opportunities for reconciliation and restoration within your family and close ones.

Why Do You Call It Supernatural Forgiveness?

I call it supernatural because you cannot naturally forgive the unforgivable by natural forgiveness and break the bondage that holds you to toxic memories. When my family helped me first, it gave me some natural relief and healing from my abuse, but it did not break the bondage of unforgiveness that is in the shadows of my life, affecting me in ways I did not even realize. When God forgave you in Christ, you received Father God's forgiveness, and now, with that actual forgiveness empowered by God Himself, you forgive the enemies of your soul. This action is initiated by your choice and enacted through you by God, so it removes the yokes of other people's sins against you.

"Be kind and compassionate to one another, forgiving each other, just as in Christ God has forgiven you."
Ephesians 4:32

Literally, with the same forgiveness, you are forgiven by God; forgive others. Everything God asks you to do is supernatural. Love with the love I have loved you with, accept with the acceptance you are accepted with and forgive with the very same forgiveness that I have forgiven you with. Christians' love, acceptance, and forgiveness all have their origin in God, empowered by the Holy Spirit of the Father.

God Pays For All Our Debts

The power of God's forgiveness is the most essential tool in God's extensive toolbox to help you overcome your past and enable a brighter future. Most people who forgive do not understand how god forgives through you. Understanding God's perspective on forgiveness is not just a theological concept but a transformative force that can radically change your life.

Many people who have been hurt often struggle with the weight of their pain, feeling trapped in cycles of resentment and bitterness. However, embracing God's desire for us to forgive, as we have been forgiven, opens the door to healing and liberation. Please read this chapter again and again until understanding comes.

Breaking The Bondage of Un-forgiveness

Forgiveness does not mean excusing or forgetting the wrongs done to us; instead, it means releasing ourselves from the chains that bind us to our past, and the persons of our past. By understanding that God actively encourages and empowers us to forgive the unforgivable, we can begin to see our wounds through His eyes—a perspective filled with love, grace, and understanding. It is like you are sitting at the table with Father God as He grants you freedom from past debts by His authority and power. That is why the Bible says—Those who are set free by the Christ are free indeed. Free in reality because God gets it done. This divine approach empowers us to let go of our burdens and step into a future filled with hope and possibility.

When we accept and grasp God's supernatural forgiveness for ourselves, extending that same grace toward others becomes more effortless.

Forgive Yourself

We often do not realize that we hold unforgiveness towards ourself! As a result of abuse of any kind we are hard on ourselves. Sometimes blame ourselves and may feel unclean or unworthy. Sometimes this is an unconscious reaction to abuse. When you ask forgiveness for yourself, the bondage of self-hatred is broken. I usually pray with people to forgive themselves once they have forgiven others first.

"For if you forgive other people when they sin against you, your heavenly Father will also forgive you." Mathew 6:14

In the 'Lord's Prayer, ' it states clearly that you should forgive others so the heavenly father can also

154

forgive you. I need to stress here that your initial forgiveness of sin when you are born again is unconditional forgiveness. But know you have been forgiven, you are expected by God, just like the King in the parable, to now forgive others because God has forgiven you of a debt you could not pay. From God's perspective, it is not optional for Christians, as we will discuss in Math 18.

Inner Peace Is The Result

This cycle of forgiveness sets you free from the past and, most importantly, cultivates inner peace. It allows us to move forward without being shackled by negative emotions or memories. Embracing this powerful tool will lead to personal growth and spiritual fulfillment —where your past no longer defines you but instead serves as a stepping stone toward your brighter future.

God Forgives for You

Forgiveness is a profound concept that often feels right in theory, yet many struggle to embody its true essence because of the deep-seated pain. We may say we forgive, but if we do not fully embrace the power of that forgiveness, we risk denying ourselves and others the healing it can bring. The key lies in understanding that our ability to forgive is intrinsically tied to the forgiveness we have received. I am going to labor this point again. The key lies in understanding that our ability to forgive is intrinsically tied to the forgiveness we have received.

When we acknowledge that we are forgiven by God, who sees beyond our flaws and mistakes, we gain access to a wellspring of grace. This divine forgiveness gives us the power to extend this compassion towards those who have wronged us. To forgive with the same God-given grace and power so you can let go of anger and resentment towards those who have broken your trust.

Ephesians 4:32 says, *"And be kind to one another, tenderhearted, forgiving one another, even AS God in Christ forgave you."*

This is easier said than done, as we all know if we have been wronged by someone who should have protected and cared for us. I have found when I first approach this subject with broken people they look away and say they cannot forgive. I kindly say I know, it was unforgivable, that is why we are going to ask God to do it for you! I invite them to reflect on their own personal experience of being forgiven by God when they did not deserve it and move them toward the understanding of God at work in them on their behalf.

Embracing this perspective transforms forgiveness from a theological concept of — 'I have to do it because God's word says I have to' — into an act of God's love, favor and grace because of God's great love for you as a good dad.

In this light, forgiving becomes not just an act of obedience or kindness but a powerful catalyst for personal freedom, growth, and deeper connections with God and others. Let us strive to forgive as we have been forgiven, recognizing the transformative power inherent in such an act.

It is God at Work Within Us

True empowered forgiveness transcends our human limitations. While we may initiate the process by making the Godly choice to forgive someone, God's forgiveness ultimately works through us, breaking the chains of unforgiveness that weigh heavily on us .

When we choose to forgive, we are not absolving or condoning others of their wrongdoings toward us or our loved ones but opening ourselves up to divine healing and transformation.

If someone has kept you chained to your past for years, do you want them to keep you chained? By forgiving them, you free yourself from their sin. The Bible says, 'be not yoked with another person's sin.'

The Initial Choice Is Yours To Make

This initial choice is crucial—it sets in motion a powerful spiritual mechanism where God's grace intervenes in our lives on our behalf. It's essential to recognize that this isn't just about letting go of bitterness; it's about inviting God's love and mercy into our wounds to heal them. In reality, these wounds cannot be healed any other way.

As we allow God's forgiveness to flow through us, we experience a release from the bondage formed by the hurt inflicted upon us by others. Through God's strength and power, we find true freedom from resentment and pain. This supernatural process empowers us to forgive and embrace a life filled with peace and joy.

Remember, empowered forgiveness isn't solely an act of will—it is an invitation for God's transformative power to heal our hearts and restore our wounded spirit and, ultimately, our health and well-being. It is a fact that many sicknesses and diseases are rooted in unforgiveness.

The Unforgiving Servant

Forgive me for driving this subject so hard, but with a lack of true understanding, people miss this powerful grace available to them.

In Chapter 18 of the Gospel of Matthew, we encounter a powerful parable that illustrates the profound nature of forgiveness. This parable serves as a compelling reminder of our responsibilities toward one another, the compassion and mercy God exercised on our behalf, and His expectations regarding our response to others.

Jesus tells the story of a king who wished to settle accounts with his servants. One servant owed an enormous debt—so great that he couldn't repay. When faced with this insurmountable debt, he pleaded for mercy, and the king, moved by compassion, forgave him entirely.

However, this same servant encountered a fellow servant who owed him a much smaller sum. Instead of extending the same grace and forgiveness he had received, he demanded repayment and showed no mercy.

This stark contrast highlights an essential truth: forgiveness is not merely an act but a reflection of our understanding and acceptance of God's grace and forgiveness in our lives. The parable challenges us to consider how often we hold onto grudges or fail to forgive those who have wronged us in seemingly minor ways compared to the enormous debt we owe God that was forgiven.

Ultimately, Jesus emphasizes that if we are unwilling to forgive others, we risk losing sight of the immense forgiveness we've been granted ourselves. This teaching encourages us to embrace forgiveness as an obligation and a pathway to healing and reconciliation.

Do We Value What God Has Done For Us?

The King judges the unforgiving servant for failing to reflect the mercy he received. Having been forgiven an immense debt, this servant turns around and refuses to extend that same grace to another who owes him a fraction of what he was forgiven.

The Consequences Are Severe

The King is disappointed in the person He forgave. The consequences are severe; he is handed over to the tormentors until his debt is repaid.

I have noticed over the years that those who do not forgive and hold deep-seated resentment and bitterness are often tormented in many ways, causing emotional sickness, insomnia, depression, and often disease.

This parable transcends its storytelling; it speaks directly to us today. When Jesus concludes with the warning that **"so will your heavenly Father do to each one of you if you do not forgive your fellow man"**

He underscores a vital truth: our capacity for forgiveness directly correlates with our understanding of God's grace toward us. It's not merely about avoiding punishment; it's about recognizing the power and privilege of forgiveness to free us from the yokes others have placed on us. But even more importantly, respectfully honoring and acknowledging what Father God has done for us. When I first heard this parable, it began a series of healings in my life and, consequently, the lives of thousands I have helped.

Un-forgiveness is Selfish, Forgiveness is Selfless

We must ask ourselves: Are we living in reflection of the grace we've received? By embracing forgiveness, we align ourselves with divine principles that foster peace and reconciliation within ourselves and others. In this light, let us strive to be conduits of grace rather than vessels of resentment, ensuring that we mirror the compassion bestowed upon us by our heavenly Father.

Forgive, and you will be Forgiven.

NOTE: In Mathew 6:14, it says, *"For if you forgive men their trespasses, your heavenly Father will also forgive you."* NKJ......This scripture underscores the profound principle that forgiveness is not merely an optional act; it is a vital choice that aligns our hearts with God's will. Forgiving others reflects our understanding of the grace and mercy of our adopted father toward us.

Forgiveness can be challenging, especially when we have been deeply hurt. However, choosing to forgive is essential for our spiritual growth and relationship with God. It frees us from the burdens of resentment and anger, allowing us to experience peace and healing. When we extend forgiveness to others, we mirror the divine forgiveness bestowed upon us—a reminder that none are beyond redemption, as hard as that may seem.

Judging Ourselves

Embracing these scriptural mandates compels us to reflect on our own lives. It is not only the big or tragic offenses against us that need to be forgiven. Remember its the small foxes that spoil the vine. Are there grudges we hold onto? Are there relationships strained by past grievances? By consciously choosing to forgive those who have wronged us in any big or small way, we obey God's command and open ourselves up to His grace in abundance.

Forgiveness is indeed a choice—a powerful one—that brings us closer to fulfilling God's purpose in our lives. Let's embrace it wholeheartedly for the sake of our own spiritual journey and well-being.

Colossians 3:13

" bearing graciously with one another, and willingly forgiving each other if one has a cause for complaint against another; just as the Lord has forgiven you, so should you forgive."

Embrace this powerful gift—allow God's forgiveness to flow through you and witness how it can improve lives, starting with yours.

CHAPTER SIXTEEN

Empty Nesters

One of the saddest things I have witnessed in marriages is the vacuum left when the kids finally leave home, and the nest is empty. For many husbands, this moment can be a harsh awakening. If parents have not nurtured a balanced, healthy relationship before their children grow up and move out, they often find themselves lost and struggling to reconnect with their wives.

As couples transition into this new phase of life, it's crucial to actively foster intimacy and understanding within their marriage. This means investing time in one another. By this, I mean they must take time out of their busy schedules to share their dreams, fears, and daily experiences without distractions. When husbands prioritize emotional connection over mere financial stability or routine gestures of affection, they create an environment where love can flourish even in an empty nest.

Many couples begin their journey as best friends in the whirlwind of early marriage, sharing laughter, dreams, and a deep emotional connection. However, as time progresses, it's too common for this love relationship to transform into a routine filled with responsibilities and obligations. Life becomes a series of tasks—managing the household, juggling work commitments, and ensuring children meet their school and extracurricular demands.

This shift can lead to a disconnect between partners who once thrived on companionship and intimacy. Vibrant conversations that once flowed effortlessly may dwindle into mundane exchanges about schedules or chores. Recognizing this transition before it becomes entrenched in daily life is crucial. Couples must actively prioritize their relationship amidst the chaos of parenting and professional duties.

Rekindling that initial bond requires intentional effort. Scheduling regular date nights or simply carving out moments for meaningful conversations can reignite the spark that once defined your partnership. Remembering that you are not just co-parents or business partners but also lovers and best friends is vital to nurturing your relationship through life's busy seasons. Embrace these opportunities to reconnect; a thriving partnership enriches your lives and sets a powerful example for your children about love and commitment.

No better training could a parent give to their children for their future than to show the enduring love that their mum and dad have for each other, no matter what life dishes out. When parents model this enduring love for their children, they provide invaluable training for future relationships and set the scene for successful marriages.

Children who witness their parents navigate life's challenges together, supporting each other through thick and thin—learn the importance of commitment and overcoming. They observe how conflicts can be resolved with grace and how affection can flourish even in tough times.

My Mum And Dad Had A Late Turnaround

It is never too late to be this example to your kids. My parents bloomed late in the marriage as they only became Christians in their 50's. They were great parents, but they grew apart over time. I always thought Dad would retire to the farm and Mum would get a condo on a beach somewhere away from Dad. But when God came into their lives, it all changed. They became best friends, traveled in a car and caravan all over Australia, worked with Hospital Christian Fellowship in different parts of the world, and led hundreds to the Lord in old age homes till they finished their run in their 90's. They were married for 66 years and went to Jesus peacefully as best friends.

The example impacted all of the siblings and showed that life can turn around even later in marriage.

Looking back over our life with the kids and many challenges, I find that our marriage and relationship have become stronger no matter what Karen and I went through. That does not mean we did not have fragile moments amid various struggles, but with God's constant help, we floated to the surface with more significant character to face the next battle that came along.

The Bible says in Romans 5 that Godly character is built in the trials of life and that God's love is shed abroad in our hearts and lives. Remember, I said success is not the absence of setbacks and failures; it's often because of them.

Love Can Conquer All

It's essential to understand that success in relationships isn't merely about avoiding setbacks or failures; rather, it often stems from how we navigate these obstacles together. Each challenge faced and overcome strengthens the bond between partners, showcasing the profound truth that true love thrives not just in moments of joy but also amid adversity. By demonstrating unwavering support and affection through thick and thin, parents instill in their children the belief that love can conquer all—an invaluable lesson that will guide them throughout their lives.

Living this example of overcoming life's multitudes of setbacks demonstrates to our children that love is not merely a feeling but an action that requires effort, patience, and dedication.

By showcasing a strong friendship at the heart of their marriage, parents lay the groundwork for their children to cultivate healthy relationships in the future. They learn that true love withstands trials and tribulations and that having a best friend by your side makes all the difference when life gets complicated. Witnessing unwavering love, there is no better training for those you can still influence than allowing them to witness it!

Again, if parents grasp this reality before it is too late, they can sail into the sunset as grandparents, hand in hand, into their old age, still being a living example of a genuine love relationship. That's what I want, do you? I still have an image of my mum and dad in Australia in their late 80s, walking hand in hand in love after 66 years of marriage.

By being ahead of this curve ball that robs so many and by taking calculated steps to deepen their bond, husbands can ensure that they don't just coexist but thrive together as partners who enjoy life side by side. It's time to break free from complacency and truly embrace what it means to be present for one another—because it's that emotional support that will keep relationships vibrant long after the children have flown the coop.

I am writing this at the age of seventy. Karen and I are empty nesters with nine grandchildren. We love our extended family, but we genuinely love the privilege of still being deeply in love with each other and facing and loving the adventure of life together.

CHAPTER SEVENTEEN

EPILOGUE

I have endeavored to touch on how dads affect every aspect of family life in good and bad ways. I have not exhausted the subject or variations of the subject, but hopefully, I exposed problems many families have with real answers from the Bible and my life experiences. The most important message I hope for people to get from this book is that there is a loving, GOOD DAD in heaven who understands your struggles and has provided a way out and the power and ability to make your way out of your deepest hurts. He also promises that after coming through to victory, the trial will only stand to make you stronger if you persevere. It is a test of your faith in God. This testing is not meant to destroy but to purify you, much like the refining of precious metals."

The scriptures below will back this claim:

- **James 1:2-4** "Count it all joy, my brothers, when you meet trials of various kinds, for you know that the testing of your faith produces perseverance."

- **Psalm 66:10**: "For you, O God, have tested us; you have tried us as silver is tried."

- **Proverbs 17:3** "The crucible is for silver, and the furnace is for gold, and the Lord tests hearts."

- **1 Peter 1:7**: "These trials come so that the proven genuineness of your faith—of greater worth than gold, which perishes even though refined by fire—may result in praise, glory, and honor when Jesus Christ is revealed."

- **James 1:2-8** "Consider it pure joy, my brothers and sisters, whenever you face trials of many kinds, because you know that the testing of your faith produces perseverance. Let perseverance finish its work so that you may be mature and complete, not lacking anything."

In all these scriptures, we are called to embrace our trials as opportunities to refine us for growth and maturity, not only for this life but for the eternal life to come. These powerful passages remind us that facing challenges is not merely a burden but a catalyst for developing perseverance. When we encounter difficulties, it's easy to succumb to despair or frustration. However, the scripture urges us to consider these moments as pure joy. This is a perspective shift that can transform how we approach adversity. Perseverance has a mighty work to make you complete and entire the word promises, so you will eventually lack nothing.

Why should we view trials with joy? Every challenge tests and strengthens our faith. Just as gold is refined through fire, life's obstacles shape our character. Embracing this mindset allows us to cultivate resilience, ultimately leading us toward spiritual maturity and completeness. You will not appreciate the reality of this promise unless your love, trust, and faith are in God to get you to a better place.

The refiner of silver was asked, "how do you know when the silver is pure?" The refiner answered, " When you can see your reflection in it." When Father God can see His reflection in our lives, the work is done. Until then brace yourself for some more refining!

That is why the book of James emphasizes the importance of letting perseverance finish its work in us. We shouldn't rush through hardships but allow them to teach us valuable lessons and refine our outlook on life. By doing so, we can emerge stronger and equipped with wisdom and understanding—qualities that enrich our personal lives and interactions with others. Remember, *'its not the beginning of the man that counts, its the end.'* This a quote by Winston Churchill from his speech at the Lord Mayor's Banquet in London on November 10, 1942. The Bible has the same thought in Ecclesiastes

7:8: **"Better is the end of a thing than the beginning thereof..."** which states the same thought. I have seen many who were faithful to God, and the faith fall away before they finished the race. We need to run this race with perseverance to the end so we win the prize.

When I look back at many of the worst moments of my life and see the hand of God now in hindsight, more than at the time of the trial, I realize my faith got me through when I could not see the way through. That's what faith is, calling the thing that is not as though it is. You do not need faith for what you have; you need faith for what you do NOT yet have! That's the test!

The Testing of your faith has resulted in something symbolically more precious than refined gold or silver. I now know that the more precious is 'who you and I become beyond the trials.' You are the workmanship, the masterpiece of God being formed in the furnace of affliction we call our life's journey.

In times of struggle, remember that you are not alone; your faith can guide you through even the toughest storms. Embrace your challenges with joy and let them lead you toward a deeper understanding of yourself and your purpose in this world. 1 Peter 1:9. *"for you are receiving the end result of your faith, the salvation of your souls."* AMEN.

INFORMATION

Thank you for reading this book. Doug will be adding more books shortly so please keep connected in the following ways;

FACEBOOK;

Facebook.com/DougStanton

facebook.com/DougstantonMinistriesInternational

WE PAGE;

www.dsmi.or

OUR DIGITAL STORE

www.dsmistore.org

Doug's Last Book It's Only Theory Until You Do it,' is also available on ;

AMAZON and APPLE BOOKs

Made in the USA
Columbia, SC
09 February 2025

53138556R00096